# Balancing Control and Flexibility in Public Budgeting

Michael Di Francesco • John Alford

# Balancing Control and Flexibility in Public Budgeting

## A New Role for Rule Variability

palgrave
macmillan

Michael Di Francesco
University of New South Wales (UNSW)
The Australia and New Zealand School of Government
Sydney, Australia

John Alford
University of Melbourne
The Australia and New Zealand School of Government
Melbourne, Australia

ISBN 978-981-10-0340-0 ISBN 978-981-10-0341-7 (eBook)
DOI 10.1007/978-981-10-0341-7

Library of Congress Control Number: 2016940842



Printed on acid-free paper

This Palgrave Macmillan imprint is published by Springer Nature
The registered company is Springer Science+Business Media Singapore Pte Ltd.

***Dedication from Michael Di Francesco***
*For Karon and Alessandro*

***Dedication from John Alford***
*For all the public servants who get things done, despite the many obstacles in their way.*

# Acknowledgments

This book is the product of ideas and explorations garnered from many conversations across the corridor that separates the authors' offices. But there have been many contributions, from near and far, that the authors have great pleasure in acknowledging.

The research on which the book is based was supported by a competitive Australia and New Zealand School of Government (ANZSOG) Research Grant (2012–2013). We are both very grateful to the School for this, and its continuing institutional backing. The project itself was superbly supported by the enthusiastic research assistance of Tom O'Connor, who himself is now practicing the art of budgetary control in the Australian Department of Finance. And during the research, officers within the Finance Department's Governance and Resource Management Group provided helpful perspectives on the design and effectiveness of budget frameworks.

A number of people generously read various incarnations of the draft work and provided valuable comments, including our ANZSOG colleagues Michael Mintrom and Sophie Yates; John Wanna, and Andrew Podger (Australian National University); Evert Lindquist (University of Victoria); Joanne Kelly (University of Sydney); and Paul Posner (George Mason University). The manuscript also benefited significantly from highly constructive suggestions of the anonymous reviewer. Refinement of the final product was made possible by the keen editorial eyes of Sophie Yates and Nicole Barling-Luke.

The authors would also like to mark personal contributions. Michael Di Francesco would like to express his appreciation and thanks to Karon, who has always been there, and to Alessandro whose fascination with numbers and counting, at the age of two-and-a-half, made writing a book about budgeting all the more important. John Alford gives special thanks to Sue Harper, who brings out the best in him.

The authors and publisher would like to acknowledge that the following material is reused with the permission of John Wiley and Sons:

Parts of Chaps. 3 and 4 are adapted from Michael Di Francesco and John Alford, 'Budget rules and flexibility in the public sector: Towards a taxonomy', *Financial Accountability & Management, 32 (2) 2016: 232–256.*

Parts of Chap. 5 are adapted from Michael Di Francesco, 'Rules and flexibility in public budgeting: The case of budget modernisation in Australia', *Australian Journal of Public Administration, 2015, doi: 10.1111/1467-8500.12156.*

The authors and publisher would like to thank Oxford University Press for permission to use Fig. 6.1 which is adapted from Fig. 2.1, 'Example of an enforcement pyramid' in Ian Ayres and John Braithwaite, *Responsive Regulation: Transcending the Deregulation Debate* (New York: Oxford University Press, 1992).

# Contents

# About the Authors

***Michael Di Francesco*** is Associate Professor in Public Sector Management and Director of the Case Program at the Australia and New Zealand School of Government and the School of Social Sciences, University of New South Wales (UNSW). He holds a PhD in public policy from the Australian National University, and has held academic appointments at the University of Melbourne, the University of Sydney and Victoria University of Wellington. Michael also has extensive senior practitioner experience in public financial management, including budget reform leadership at the NSW Treasury, and many expert advisory appointments at the International Monetary Fund and World Bank. Michael has published numerous articles and chapters, and has twice been a recipient of the Sam Richardson Award for the most influential article in the *Australian Journal of Public Administration*.

***John Alford*** is Professor of Public Sector Management at the Australia and New Zealand School of Government and the Melbourne Business School, University of Melbourne. He holds a PhD and MBA from the Melbourne Business School, where he has taught since 1988, and has held visiting fellowships at the Australian National University and Utrecht University. John is an international authority in the areas of public value and client-organization relationships. He has published many articles in international journals, and two books with Palgrave Macmillan: *Engaging Public Sector Clients* (2009), winner of the 2011 American Society for Public Administration's SPAR Award for the Best Public Administration Book, and (with Janine O'Flynn) *Rethinking Public Service Delivery* (2012), winner of the 2013 Academy of Management (Public/Nonprofit Division) Best Book Award.

# List of Figures

# List of Tables

CHAPTER 1

# Introduction

**Abstract** This chapter introduces a neglected but core question in contemporary public management theory and practice: how can public budgeting be set up to balance the central oversight need for standardization and the local situational need for flexibility? It surveys how this tension is intensified by increasingly complex policy environments and tightened fiscal conditions. After noting the disappointing impacts of flexibility-oriented budget reforms over the last 30 years, the chapter outlines a new approach to conceptualizing budget control and flexibility, as well as the means by which budget-rule variability might strike a more sustainable balance.

In the field of management these days, 'flexibility' is usually regarded as a good thing. It contrasts with its assumed antonym of 'inflexibility' or 'rigidity'. This is particularly true in the private sector, as leading business figures bemoan the inflexibility of labor markets or the rigidity of government regulation. But it also resonates increasingly in the public sector, as government organizations struggle to adapt to today's more complex problems and more turbulent environments with what they see as yesterday's sclerotic structures and processes. At least implicitly, these organizations are increasingly being called to account for how well they meet these challenges—most notably we hold them responsible for delivering outcomes mandated by the government. Enhancing flexibility is therefore seen as a means of enabling public organizations to meet their accountability for achieving results.



M. Di Francesco, J. Alford, *Balancing Control and Flexibility in Public Budgeting*, DOI 10.1007/978-981-10-0341-7_1

Budget systems, of course, are key means of operationalizing government accountability (Bandy 2015: 43–54; Funnell et al. 2012: 12–21, 42–64). They prescribe rules for the allocation, spending, accumulation, transferring, and accounting of public money, and breaches of these rules, when brought out into the light by the legislature's committees, auditors, or the media, are seen more or less as betrayals of the public trust. In every government these rules are superintended through some form of 'central finance agency', whether Her Majesty's Treasury in the executive-dominated parliamentary system of the UK or the Office of Management and Budget (OMB) within the Presidency of the intentionally fragmented separation-of-powers system in the USA (Guess and Leloup 2010: 8–30).[1]

However, flexibility can also be contrasted in the public sector context with another concept of enduring significance: 'consistency'. Its guiding value is the most common form of fairness—the equitable treatment of citizens—typically manifested in a focus on procedural fairness. This has been sustained historically through a cultural orientation, often unduly stereotyped, to 'rule following'; more fundamentally it also rests on constitutional foundations, which are borne of the public's expectation that their governments should be accountable to them for how they marshal and deploy the resources which citizens have bestowed on them, whether voluntarily or compulsorily.

But this attention to process increasingly jostles with organizational efforts to achieve results. Further, achieving results is often seen to be best facilitated by granting government bodies and their managers some level of autonomy—and, hence, flexibility—to determine and implement the most effective means to achieve mandated ends. These differing logics have always been present, but the relationship between them became even more salient with the rise of the New Public Management (NPM) from the start of the 1980s, which gave impetus to the shift from compliance-based processes to performance-based results, especially in relatively routine and high volume public sector tasks (Pollitt and Bouckaert 2004: 6–20; for the classic account see Hood 1991).

Now, however, the need for flexibility has burgeoned beyond the requirements of the managerialist routines, and indeed those routines are themselves being queried. One reason has been the emergence of more complex issues and increasingly turbulent environments, which collectively we will call 'nonroutine problems'. In this context, budgeting and financial management processes in government are inevitably caught between contending institutional imperatives for responsiveness and consistency: the public's expectations that the problems stemming from growing interdependencies and disruption will be addressed with the help of some flexibility, and the same public's expectations that the resources used by government to tackle those problems will be managed efficiently and fairly (Behn 2001; Kettl 2009). More to the point, specific types of routines, such as budgeting and financial management rules and their purported rigidity, are quite commonly singled out as a—if not *the*—'critical barrier' for public organizations in terms of the operational agility required to respond collaboratively to complex problems (O'Flynn 2014: 4; see also McDaid 2012; Mitchell and Thurmaier 2011).

This is the subject of this book. Its core question is *how can public budgeting be set up to balance the 'central' oversight need for standardization and the 'local' situational need for flexibility*? In other words, can public budgeting be made more flexible without diminishing the capacity of government to ensure public money is devoted to the purposes it has mandated? There are, we believe, two important reasons why it is timely to ask the question. The first is to explain unrealized intentions. The period since the mid-1980s has been marked internationally by historically significant levels of public sector budget modernization. Under the aegis of the 'new' public financial management—and across both advanced and less developed economies—a broad range of interlocking fiscal control, budget management and financial accounting reforms have been prosecuted largely in the name of *devolved resourcing and expanded managerial autonomy* (Allen et al. 2013; Schick 2013). That budget processes *continue* to be perceived as one of the key 'brakes' on government flexibility is perplexing, and ultimately something of an indictment of the impact of these public management reform efforts.

The second motivation is about responding to extant fiscal pressures. Not least as a consequence of increased complexity—in this instance of global finance markets—many of the same governments who engineered budget modernization are now contending with the unprecedented fiscal legacy of the 'Great Recession' of 2008–2009. Faced with the prospect of imminent collapse in ailing banking systems, and the attendant risk of social and economic disorder, governments across the OECD, but particularly in the USA and the euro zone, were compelled to recapitalize financial systems on a massive scale, with serious impacts on their deficit and debt positions. The response, while in no way universal, has been an internationally sanctioned agenda of 'fiscal consolidation' (or 'austerity') that seeks to cut structural expenditures, such as entitlement-driven programs like social security (Posner and Blondal 2012: 11–17). Flexibility, of course, is not usually associated with the sharp budget contractions of austerity, which tends to be closely coupled with tight central control of financial inputs (Johansson and Siverbo 2014: 272). So, it has to be asked, if public sector reformers were unable to get traction on flexibility with devolved financial management in the comparatively buoyant fiscal age of the 1990s and early 2000s, are the prospects for doing so any brighter in the current highly distressed budgetary circumstances?

We think there remains considerable scope for a rebalancing of control and flexibility in key aspects of public budgeting. In part this is framed by the *operational* capabilities required to respond to greater prevalence of 'nonroutine' problems, whether they be exogenous (such as coordinating emergency responses to an economic crisis) or endogenous (as with customizing services to the increasingly segmented needs and preferences of the public). And, in part, it is framed by the *policy* imperatives residing in the current austerity, to better target fiscal consolidation and, within top-down ceilings, to entrust spending departments and managers with *genuine* authority to vary the way the reduced resources are applied (see, for example, OECD 2011: 1–2). From the point of view of a central finance agency, there are natural tendencies to see these types of outcomes as a zero-sum issue: there can be more flexibility and less control, or vice versa, but not both. As we will see, it is also true that budget modernization has sought to capitalize on opportunities to enhance flexibility while ensuring spending parameters are observed: in fact, the whole shift under NPM to give managers more of a say about how results are to be achieved within centrally imposed financial and performance limits can be understood precisely in these terms. However, as we shall also explore below, this form of budget and managerial flexibility struggles to relate to nonroutine problems.

The argument of the book proceeds in six parts. In Chap. 2 we introduce the lightning rod for enhanced flexibility in government: the rise of nonroutine problems and the apparent misalignment of public organizational structures and capabilities. Different and expanding forms of policy complexity and environmental turbulence are challenging public officials—elected and appointed alike—to become *more* collaborative, agile, and resilient in the way they respond to nonroutine problems. We survey the nature of these problems, and catalogue the most common forms of nonroutine responses. In Chap. 3, we narrow our focus to the role of public budgeting practices in hindering organizational responses to nonroutine problems; in particular, we illustrate how salient features of budgeting can inhibit the conditions for collaboration across government, and between government and nongovernment actors. To anchor this discussion, Chap. 3 sets out a working definition of 'budget flexibility', which we explain in multidimensional terms corresponding to the level of decision-making authority and, crucially, the scope for rule variability across the phases of the budget cycle. This sets the stage for a detailed consideration of budgeting and an interrogation of the push and pull of budget rules.

We commence Chap. 4 with a high level survey of the centrality of budgeting to organizational control, applying cross-disciplinary lenses to compare approaches to budgeting in the public and private sectors (a contrast that is not nearly as great as commonly supposed). This presages a revisiting of the traditional model of public budgeting and financial management—which emphasizes control of and accountability for financial inputs—so as to better understand why its practices and cultural orientation remain so prevalent in government. In doing so, we develop a taxonomy to characterize general 'budget rules' that delineate budget execution tasks in the public sector, and seek to explain how they operate through key properties of control. To illustrate this, we focus on two of the most prominent rules, the 'annuality' and 'purpose' of spending. We then describe what high flexibility might look like for each of the budget rules, and speculate on what the implications are for sustainable rule modification. Our context is primarily the political institutions, norms and practices of Westminster-style parliamentary systems, such as Australia and the UK, but we contend that the taxonomy has much broader application and relevance.[2]

Chapter 5 of the book integrates the taxonomy and the dimensions of budget flexibility to provide an extended application of the framework to a discrete episode of budget modernization. The aim of this chapter is to illustrate how the trade-offs between control and flexibility have manifested themselves in practice. After surveying the features of NPM-inspired budget modernization in an international context, and specifically the design intent for 'flexibility' residing within these schemes, we apply the taxonomy by analyzing the impact of rule interactions in the case of performance-based budget reforms in Australia over the period 1983–2010. Over three phases of restructuring, we identify four legacy reforms and show how the trace patterns of the budget rules can be discerned in the design, interaction, and redesign of the four reforms. We argue that the rules continue to exert strong influence on budgetary behavior.

Whilst Chap. 5 serves to temper expectations for what conventional approaches to rule modification can achieve in expanding budget flexibility, Chap. 6 sets out a more optimistic assessment of the practical opportunities that might be available to reformers. We articulate the role of 'rule variability'—the institutionalized capacity to vary the way rules are applied within basic rule sets—as a viable option for recalibrating aspects of control and flexibility in budgeting. This approach is situated in the evolving context of the regulatory relationship between central finance agencies and spending departments. We discharge two conventional role types for the central finance agency—persistent 'command-and-control' and the more short-lived 'facilitator' roles—and concentrate on the potential of two quite radical role descriptions: experimentation with 'sanctioned rule-breaking' and the novel application of 'earned autonomy' as an internal-to-government form of 'responsive regulation'. Each is assessed in terms of its capacity to optimize the two dimensions of budget flexibility. We conclude that each has possibilities and limitations, but that their efficacy is likely to vary from one situation to another, raising the possibility of a contingency—that is, a distinct 'rule variability'—approach to budget flexibility.

## Notes

1. There is no standardized terminology for executive government central agencies responsible for budget and financial management functions, with variations including 'central budget agency', 'finance ministry', 'finance department' and 'treasury' (Wanna 2003: xxviii). We use the term 'central finance agency' as a convenient shorthand. The functions of these agencies are discussed in more detail later in the book.
2. We define Westminster-style parliamentary systems as those broadly characterized by the executive government being formed by the party (or coalition of parties) holding a majority in the lower (popular) house of parliament; responsible cabinet government in which the executive branch is drawn from the parliament and is directly accountable to the parliament through the conventions of individual and collective ministerial responsibility; and where the bureaucratic arm of the executive comprises a professional and 'politically neutral' civil service (Rhodes et al. 2009: 4–9). These systems include the UK, Australia, Canada, New Zealand, India, Ireland, and Malaysia. Whilst the practices and conventions underpinning these systems are constantly evolving, they can be said to differ from presidential separation-of-powers systems—most notably the USA—in respect of their strength of party cohesion, recruitment of (policy generalist) cabinet members from the legislature, and the centralization of both legislative power and accountability in the executive (Weaver and Rockman 1993: 11–16).

## References


Allen, R., R. Hemming, and B. Potter. 2013. The meaning, content and objectives of public financial management. In *The international handbook of public financial management*, ed. R. Allen, R. Hemming, and B. Potter, 1–12. New York: Palgrave Macmillan.

Bandy, G. 2015. *Financial management and accountability in the public sector*, 2nd ed. London: Routledge.

Behn, R. 2001. *Rethinking democratic accountability*. Washington, DC: Brookings Institution.

Funnell, W., K. Cooper, and J. Lee. 2012. *Public sector accounting and accountability in Australia*, 2nd ed. Sydney: UNSW Press.

Guess, G.M., and L.T. Leloup. 2010. *Comparative public budgeting: Global perspectives on taxing and spending*. Albany, NY: State University of New York Press.

Hood, C. 1991. A public management for all seasons? *Public Administration* 69(1): 3–19.

Johansson, T., and S. Siverbo. 2014. The appropriateness of tight budget control in public sector organizations facing budget turbulence. *Management Accounting Research* 25(4): 271–283.

Kettl, D. 2009. *The next government of the United States*. New York: W.W. Norton.

McDaid, D. 2012. Joint budgeting: Can it facilitate intersectoral action? In *Intersectoral governance for health in all policies: Structures, actions and experiences*, ed. D. McQueen, M. Wismar, V. Lin, C. Jones, and M. Davies, 111–127. Copenhagen: World Health Organization.

Mitchell, D., and K. Thurmaier. 2011. Toward a theory of budgeting for collaboration. Paper presented at the Public Management Research Conference, Maxwell School of Citizenship and Public Affairs, Syracuse University, NY, 2–4 June 2011.

O'Flynn, J. 2014. Crossing boundaries in public management and policy: An introduction. In *Crossing boundaries in public management and policy: The international experience*, ed. J. O'Flynn, D. Blackman, and J. Halligan, 3–10. London: Routledge.

OECD. 2011. *Reforming the institutional framework for budgeting*. OECD Working Party of Senior Budget Officials. Paris: OECD.

Pollitt, C., and G. Bouckaert. 2004. *Public management reform: A comparative analysis*, 2nd ed. Oxford: Oxford University Press.

Posner, P., and J. Blondal. 2012. Democracies and deficits: Prospects for fiscal responsibility in democratic nations. *Governance* 25(1): 11–34.

Rhodes, R., J. Wanna, and P. Weller. 2009. *Comparing Westminster*. Oxford: Oxford University Press.

Schick, A. 2013. Reflections on two decades of public financial management reforms. In *Public financial management and its emerging architecture*, ed. M. Cangiano, T. Curristine, and M. Lazare, 21–76. Washington, DC: International Monetary Fund.

Wanna, J. 2003. Introduction: The changing role of central budget agencies. In *The reality of budgetary reform in OECD nations: Trajectories and consequences*, ed. J. Wanna, L. Jensen, and J. De Vries, xxiii–xxxviii. Cheltenham: Edward Elgar.

Weaver, R. Kent, and B.A. Rockman. 1993. Assessing the effects of institutions. In *Do institutions matter? Government capabilities in the United States and abroad*, ed. R. Kent Weaver and B.A. Rockman, 1–41. Washington, DC: The Brookings Institution.

CHAPTER 2

# Nonroutine Problems and Flexibility

**Abstract** This chapter surveys the imperatives for enhanced flexibility in government, including the rise of nonroutine problems and the misalignment of public organizational structures and capabilities. It explores how different and expanding forms of policy complexity and environmental turbulence are challenging public officials to become more collaborative, agile, and resilient in the way they respond to nonroutine problems. The chapter surveys the nature of nonroutine problems and catalogues the most common forms of nonroutine responses deployed by public organizations.

## 2.1 The Nature of Nonroutine Problems

The urge to standardize and routinize has historically been strong in public administration, underpinned by the Weberian archetype of impersonal rule application through bureaucratic form (Weber 1946: 196–204, 212–216). Operationally, it took shape as consistency of processes, and sustained organizations' capacity to produce large-volume uniform services efficiently. Normatively, it was a natural corollary of the need for equity in the application of rules. Consequently public sector organizations have tended to orient themselves to what we might call the routine services of government (Kettl 2009). This did not abate with the emergence of NPM from the early 1980s. Its adoption of multiyear corporate planning, of program budgeting—usually corresponding to a 'product format'—and



M. Di Francesco, J. Alford, *Balancing Control and Flexibility in Public Budgeting*, DOI 10.1007/978-981-10-0341-7_2

of measurement of performance was recognized quite early as having the practical effect of further 'routinizing' public services (Considine 1988).

But at the same time as government organizations have sharpened their focus on routine services, they have been confronted by increasingly problematic issues in the social and natural world around them, to which their routine processes are not well suited. We readily acknowledge that organizations, both public and private, have long had to strike a balance between routine and nonroutine decision-making repertoires and structures (see, for example, March and Simon 1958; Cyert and March 1963), but it is arguable that the speed and complexity of change, propelled today by digital technologies, is now placing a greater premium on the capacity to make *non*routine decisions and deliver *non*routine services. These nonroutine problems take several different but interrelated forms.

First, there are *complex* problems, in which different issues, each the responsibility of a particular department, are entangled with each other, or where the same issue straddles several departments. Either way, the net effect of this interdependency is that departments find they have to interact with other departments and seek their collaboration or, at the very least, acquiescence. No single department has the authority, resources, information, or capabilities to deal with the problem on its own. The most extreme form of complex problems is the '*wicked* problem'—such as the multifaceted social, economic, and regulatory effects of illicit drug use—which is intractable, involves multiple conflicting interests, and is inherently resistant to clear definition and solution (see Head and Alford 2015).

A second kind of nonroutine problem is a *crisis*: an unexpected event or situation that generates uncertainty, is a threat to the organization or society, and calls for urgent and/or complex change. This usually means that goals must change and resources be redirected in a major way. Natural disasters, such as the 2011 earthquake that devastated the central business district of Christchurch in New Zealand, are an obvious example. Finally, related to crisis is *turbulence*, in which the organization is buffeted spasmodically but continuously by a series of difficult events. This turbulence can, for instance, take the form of political conflict that arises from problematic change, such as the disruptive social and economic effects of new digital technologies that fuel the growing 'peer-to-peer' sharing economy. It almost always means that settled understandings about political positions, decision processes, or resource distributions are challenged.

## 2.2 The Forms of Nonroutine Responses

It is important to stress that these types of problems are real; they arise from objective conditions in the environment surrounding the organization, or what organizational theorists would call the 'task environment' (Dill 1958; cf. Leonard and Moore 2012). All of them call for changes—short- and/or long-term—in policies, structures, resources, and processes. They dictate that government makes decisions out of the ordinary and fashions new ways of operating. We will call these responses 'nonroutine governance' or 'nonroutine management'. Several types have emerged in the last couple of decades.

Most noteworthy is 'collaboration' or 'networked governance', where one or more government agencies deliberate and work together with other government agencies, private firms, or nonprofits on a particular set of tasks.[1] Typically it involves the participating parties sharing the decision-making, or the actual work, or both (Donahue and Zeckhauser 2011; Sullivan and Skelcher 2002). Various configurations fit within this category. 'Joined up government' or 'whole-of-government' arrangements entail government agencies working together. Another configuration involves a public sector organization working with nonprofit providers and/or private contractors. Sometimes these are framed as 'public-private partnerships' (PPPs), often governed by classical contracts, in which the government defines what is to be done and the provider performs the work, with the main differences from contracting residing in the arrangements for the funding of the project and ownership of the assets created in the process (Hodge and Greve 2005). At their most elaborate, collaborations can involve multiparty networks with complex governance arrangements.

The literature shows in abundance that successful collaboration between organizations relies on certain conditions, which the participating actors need to work at creating or sustaining (Alford and O'Flynn 2012; Huxham and Vangen 2005). One is agreement on purposes. This could be facilitated by the organizations involved having common interests. Although it is more likely organizations will have different goals and almost certainly differing interests, it is well recognized that different but complementary purposes can form the basis for agreed goals, dovetailed in a 'win/win' configuration, and made even stronger by the interdependency that underlies the complementarity of their purposes (Vangen and Huxham 2012; Lax and Sebenius 1986). A second condition is mutual commitment between the parties. At a minimum, this entails a degree of reciprocal respect and even concern for the other partners by each partner. More solidly, it might also entail each party making a tangible self-commitment, by signaling through some action that they have rendered themselves with no choice but to collaborate—for example, by contributing a nontrivial quantity of resources to the project on which the collaboration is to work, or signing an agreement including undertakings which must be met.

Another major condition is mutual trust between the parties. Trust is recognized as an alternative to the carrots and sticks wielded in classical contracting (Alford and O'Flynn 2012; deHoog 1990). It involves each party developing confidence that the other parties will 'do the right thing' in situations where it is vulnerable to their actions. Following Gouldner's (1960) famous 'norm', building up trust stems from a pattern of mutual positive gestures, examples of which might be sharing information, bending (but not breaking) rules, or not taking advantage of unpredictable circumstances. At a minimum, it demands that organizations and those representing them in interorganizational dealings deliver on what they promise. Repeated reneging on undertakings undermines the credibility of organizational representatives.

This process of building trust takes considerable time, since each positive gesture is not scheduled in an orderly fashion, but rather arises haphazardly in the course of organizational life (Covey 2006). This makes it susceptible to changes in personnel, policies, procedures, and resources. For staff acting on behalf of their department in a collaborative process with other organizations, it is also important that they have sufficient autonomy to make judgments about appropriate trust-enhancing offerings. However, these collaborative interactions tend to be constrained by the legitimate accountability requirements that surround public sector programs and organizations. Rules relating to procurement, human resources, and, of course, budgeting and financial management, tend to affect the extent to which organizational representatives can make positive gestures and deliver on undertakings.

Another emerging response to nonroutine problems is to seek to create agile organizations, that is, public agencies that can respond quickly to major and rapid changes in their circumstances. These responses include not only changes to the 'hardware' of the organization—its structures and systems—but also to its cultural 'software' (Beinhocker 2006). Typical proposals for enabling governments to become more agile call for the development of three types of capacity: to scan and thereby spot emerging trends and issues; to respond flexibly at both a tactical and strategic level; and to shape by understanding how to drive change in the external environment to influence future opportunities and minimize risk. Related to organizational agility is the notion of resilience: the capacity to adapt in a positive manner to a massive failure caused by a disaster or emergency. Thus, when the Australian state of Victoria experienced the disaster of the Black Saturday bushfires in 2009, with 173 dead, thousands of homes burnt, and major infrastructure destroyed, a high level of resilience was called for to restore not only physical infrastructure but also community fabric (Leonard and Howitt 2010).

Significantly, both agility and resilience can be assisted by collaborative measures. Collaboration can help in pooling learnings and solutions in crisis situations, by virtue of the fact that consultation and communication are inherent in its modus operandi. To the extent that it entails the building of trust, it is likely to enable speedier responses in multiparty emergency response or recovery processes, as Covey's phrase 'the speed of trust' underscores (Covey 2006).

These responses to nonroutine problems—collaboration, agility, and resilience—all necessitate a degree of flexibility in the structures and processes of government. But prima facie, they tend on the whole to have a different logic to the standard operating procedures of routine government. Most of the rules, procedures and systems that make 'business as usual' functional are likely to constrain the kinds of actions and behaviors that nonroutine problems require.[2] To that extent they limit the flexibility of government organizations in their efforts to collaborate or to exercise agility or resilience. This is especially true of the primary focus of this book: the flexibility of budgeting and financial management systems.

## Notes

1. 'Collaboration' is perhaps the most common term to describe working across organizational and sectoral boundaries. The focus here on collaboration is intended to exemplify arrangements *where flexibility is considered important* to the effectiveness of public policy design and service delivery outcomes. For a survey of the different types see Alford and O'Flynn (2012: 113–124).
2. It should not go unnoticed that the advancement and diffusion of digital technologies, as one of the drivers of much contemporary social and economic

disruption, *may* also create more scope for decision-makers to achieve a better balance between routine and nonroutine responses and structures. One example is the way that social media can be deployed to mobilize government and civil society responses to natural disaster and terrorism emergencies.

## References


Alford, J., and J. O'Flynn. 2012. *Rethinking public service delivery: Managing with external providers*. Basingstoke: Palgrave Macmillan.

Beinhocker, E. 2006. The adaptable corporation. *McKinsey Quarterly* 2: 76–87.

Considine, M. 1988. The corporate management framework as administrative science: A critique. *Australian Journal of Public Administration* 47(1): 4–18.

Covey, S. 2006. *The speed of trust: The one thing that changes everything*. New York: The Free Press.

Cyert, R.M., and J. March. 1963. *A behavioral theory of the firm*. Englewood Cliffs, NJ: Prentice-Hall.

DeHoog, R. 1990. Competition, negotiation or cooperation: Three models for service contracting. *Administration & Society* 22(3): 317–340.

Dill, W.R. 1958. Environment as an influence on managerial autonomy. *Administrative Science Quarterly* 2(4): 409–443.

Donahue, J., and R. Zeckhauser. 2011. *Collaborative governance: Private roles for public goals in turbulent times*. Princeton, NJ: Princeton University Press.

Gouldner, A. 1960. The norm of reciprocity: A preliminary statement. *American Sociological Review* 25(2): 161–178.

Head, B., and J. Alford. 2015. Wicked problems: Implications for public policy and management. *Administration & Society* 47(6): 711–739.

Hodge, G., and C. Greve. 2005. *The challenge of public-private partnerships: Learning from international experience*. Cheltenham: Edward Elgar.

Huxham, C., and S. Vangen. 2005. *Managing to collaborate: The theory and practice of collaborative advantage*. London: Routledge.

Kettl, D. 2009. *The next government of the United States*. New York: W.W. Norton.

Lax, D., and J. Sebenius. 1986. *The manager as negotiator: Bargaining for cooperation and competitive gain*. New York: Free Press.

Leonard, H.B., and A.M. Howitt. 2010. Organising response to extreme emergencies: The Victorian bushfires of 2009. *Australian Journal of Public Administration* 69(4): 372–386.

Leonard, H.B., and M.H. Moore. 2012. Pursuing public value: Frameworks for strategic analysis and action. In *Ports in a storm: Public management in a turbulent world*, ed. J.D. Donahue and M.H. Moore, 84–115. Washington, DC: Brookings Institution Press.

March, J.G., and H.A. Simon. 1958. *Organizations*. New York: Wiley.

Sullivan, H., and C. Skelcher. 2002. *Working across boundaries: Collaboration in public services*. Basingstoke: Palgrave Macmillan.

Vangen, S., and C. Huxham. 2012. The tangled web: Unravelling the principle of common goals in collaborations. *Journal of Public Administration Research and Theory* 22(4): 731–760.

Weber, M. 1946. *From Max Weber: Essays in sociology*. Trans. and ed. H.H. Gerth and C. Wright Mills. New York: Oxford University Press.

CHAPTER 3

# Flexibility, Inflexibility, and Budgeting

**Abstract** This chapter focuses on the ways public budgeting practices can hinder organizational responses to nonroutine problems. It illustrates how salient features of budgeting can inhibit the conditions for collaboration across government, and between government and nongovernment actors. To anchor this discussion, the chapter sets out a working definition of budget flexibility, which is explained in multidimensional terms corresponding to the level of decision-making authority and the scope for rule variability across the phases of the budget cycle.

## 3.1 Budgeting as an Inhibitor of Flexibility

Budget rules are usually seen as 'hard' factors in the management of organizations; they derive their force from the simple fact that they govern the key resource for implementing government priorities: money. To the extent that budgeting does entail the application of rules—which after all are authoritative statements of what may or may not be done[1]—it can be seen as inhibiting flexibility and hence collaboration, resilience, and/or agility. This can happen in four main ways, intended or unintended.

First, budget rules[2] *directly* inhibit flexibility by specifically prescribing or proscribing where, upon what, when, how, and how much public money can be allocated, spent, accumulated, or transferred, and who has authority to permit or prohibit these actions (Jones and Thompson 1986). These basic control properties will receive detailed treatment in Chap. 4.



M. Di Francesco, J. Alford, *Balancing Control and Flexibility in Public Budgeting*, DOI 10.1007/978-981-10-0341-7_3

Second, the rules are more likely to constrict flexibility if they are cast in ex ante rather than ex post terms (Thompson 1993). Ex ante rules entail the regulator controlling the inputs and/or processes before or during the activity being regulated. By contrast, ex post rules are applied after the event, so that in the meantime the regulatee has room to deviate. As we will discuss later, the shift from ex ante to ex post control, especially as it applies to internal controls, is one of the defining trends in international public financial management reform (Ruffner and Sevilla 2004). For example, traditional financial control systems, where payments are approved prior to commitment by a central controller (sometimes located in the central finance agency), have largely been replaced with devolved management information systems to authorize transactions that are externally audited after payment is made.

Third, budget rules can make it more difficult for government organizations to mount responses to nonroutine situations. Collaboration often requires devoting funds to a purpose transcending the organizational units involved. This means two or more organizations must consent to reallocate funds to the agreed purpose through what is known as 'joint budgeting' (McDaid 2012). Joint budgeting can take a range of forms—see Table 3.1 below—but the most common structures are *aligned budgets* (where organizations agree to assign part of their budget in support of a shared purpose while retaining full responsibility for their own contributions) and *pooled budgets* (where organizations each agree to contribute to a single fund to achieve a shared purpose, and the fund is either managed by a third party or governed by a formal funding agreement) (Raine and Watt 2013: 880–886). Ultimately, as we will see, budget rules usually mandate that one entity is the 'budget holder' for a particular allocation, which means there needs to be either a high level of trust between the partners, or, as in the case of pooled budgets, a mechanism to safeguard the over-riding purpose, especially when circumstances change (which is highly likely in the public sector) (Mitchell and Thurmaier 2011: 5–8). To the extent that budget rules limit the degree to which funds can be thus reallocated, they constrain the basic wherewithal for implementing the purposes of the collaboration. Either way, they complicate the ability of funding parties to contribute their fair share or to honor undertakings, which in turn undermines trust.

These types of issues have been encountered in a number of OECD countries, where over the last two decades experimentation with joint budgeting has been used to structure service delivery, especially in the health

**Table 3.1** Alternative models for joint budgeting in government[a]

| *Model* | *Description* | *Mechanisms* | *Accountabilities* |
|---|---|---|---|
| Central or policy-oriented budget | A single fund for shared purpose(s) (usually policy sectoral)<br>Funds are allocated to a designated organization | Type 1: A single fund for shared purposes is managed and/or allocated by the designated organization<br>Type 2: Central government 'ring-fences' funds for shared purposes and organizations may submit 'joint proposals' through the budget process | Type 1: The designated organization is directly accountable for managing and reporting on use of funds<br>Type 2: A lead agency submits a joint budget proposal which is supported by a funding agreement (refer Pooled budget Lead Agency Model) |
| Pooled budget | A single fund for a shared purpose (usually program or objective specific)<br>Two or more organizations contribute funds from their own existing budgets | A funding agreement specifies purposes and the financial responsibilities of partner organizations<br>Type 1: Pooled budget may be 'owned' by one organization<br>Type 2: Pooled budget may be 'oversighted' by one organization without direct control or subject to veto by partner organizations | Accountabilities for Types 1 and 2 can take two forms:<br>Lead Agency Model: A lead organization is directly accountable for managing and reporting on use of pooled funds<br>Third Party Model: A separate organization is established and is directly accountable for managing and reporting on use of pooled funds |
| Aligned budget | Two or more organizations agree to assign funds from their own existing budgets for a shared purpose (usually program or objective specific) | Type 1: A formal or informal agreement may specify purposes and contributions from each organization<br>Type 2: Each organization may decide on a 'best endeavors' basis how their existing budgets will be deployed | Each organization is directly accountable for managing and reporting on the use of its own (contributed) funds |

[a]Drawing on Raine and Watt (2013: 883) and McDaid (2012: 114)

and community sectors (McDaid 2012). A good example comes from the Manchester North West Resettlement Consortium (NWRC) in the United Kingdom (Raine et al. 2011; Raine and Watt 2013). The NWRC was initially a pilot project to encourage integrated working between the youth justice system, children's services and other important services in disadvantaged local authority areas with the aim of reducing re-offending by juveniles. Young offenders coming out of custody within the area received enhanced resettlement support, including mentoring, extra assistance with accommodation, as well as education, training, and employment. Four Greater Manchester local authorities were involved in the collaboration, working with one another and other nongovernment stakeholders. The NWRC used an 'aligned budget' model: authorities contributed their own resources, although initially funding was supplemented by a central government grant. Whilst 'pooled budgets' were much the preferred funding mechanism among partners, an aligned model was adopted because some local authorities were concerned about 'surrendering control of their budgets', as a key figure in the program observed:

> we have a [re-offending] prevention budget—but have never succeeded—everybody's budget is too tied up … (We) all have got different accounting and report back arrangements. (Raine et al. 2011: 54–55; Raine and Watt 2013: 891)

In this case, not only was a lack of trust between partners at the beginning of the project identified as a key obstacle—even though this lessened over time—but so too was the incompatibility of the financial management and reporting systems used by each authority.

A variation on this problem is that sometimes programs can be framed in a way that does not quite fit with the 'territory' to which the collaborative enterprise is devoted. In other words, not only are there organizational 'silos', but these silos operate to a logic that is partly out of sync with the purposes of the collaboration. Within its own jurisdiction, each party allocates some funds that contribute to the agreed purpose, but also one of them contributes some funds that are about a purpose that only that party supports. An instructive example comes from Australia (Halligan 2008). The Australians Working Together (AWT) initiative sought to bring services from three departments into 'one stop shops' under Centrelink, the national social services delivery agency, in an attempt to disrupt organizational silos. However, the funding arrangements still entailed appropriation of funds to participating departments within the existing program structure, who in turn passed the money on to Centrelink. The consequence was that although there was an effort to set up an array of cross-agency service channels, in fact all but two of the AWT measures were delivered solely by individual agencies (Halligan 2008: 41–48).

Fourth, because it often applies to activities or purposes longer than a year, collaboration can also be impeded if the parties involved are unable to reallocate monies from one time period to another. For example, this might be the case where it turns out that only modest spending is required in the start-up year of a project, as the initial groundwork is less expensive than forecast, requiring the bulk of dedicated funding to be allocated over the subsequent operational years; or perhaps in circumstances of urgency or opportunity that might require funding additional to that originally planned being brought forward from later budget years. To the extent that budget rules can limit these movements, they hamper multiyear projects. In other situations, for instance, governments may provide 'time-limited' grants for collaborative ventures, the expiration of which shifts the funding burden onto subordinate partners (say, nongovernment organizations or local governments) (McDaid 2012: 118–119). Acting in tandem with these complications, collaboration can be impeded where the parties at the 'coal-face' of the partnership lack budgetary decision authority, and are thereby constrained in the extent to which they can allocate or reallocate monies between organizations, programs, or time periods. In practice, organizational representatives at the 'boundary' must either return to their superiors for approval to make a change (O'Flynn et al. 2011) or resort to informal 'workarounds' to circumvent rules (Campbell 2012).

These issues of 'periodicity' and 'decision rights' are exemplified in another Australian case. Indigenous Coordination Centres (ICCs) were created to provide a 'one stop shop' for whole-of-government delivery of both mainstream and indigenous-specific services to Indigenous (Aboriginal and Torres Strait Islander) communities across Australia (O'Flynn et al. 2011). Although the federal Department of Families, Housing, Community Services and Indigenous Affairs (FaHCSIA) was the lead agency responsible for Indigenous affairs, there were 210 indigenous-specific programs administered by more than 40 agencies across 17 portfolios. FaHCSIA did not have the authority to direct staff from other agencies in their activities. The high numbers of programs and agencies involved in indigenous service delivery, and the lack of lead agency authority, necessitated agencies entering into large numbers of funding agreements in order to integrate services. A review by the Australian National Audit Office (ANAO) into federal government coordination arrangements for indigenous programs noted that although 'relevant funding agreements would ideally take place at the level at which they are approved as well as early in the design of programs', the ICCs provided 'little authority for decisions on funding agreements to be taken locally' as 'the people on the ground aren't the decision makers' (ANAO 2012: 80). One frustrated FaHCSIA manager captured the systemic experience with financial delegations to ICCs thus:

> There's ... the structural problems that everyone faces ... around the funding agreements ... really inhibiting for anyone ... and that certainly has happened [on] numerous occasions where ... people have been able to say, 'well I think we can do that' and ... then going away and finding the actual delegate says, 'no' ... and yet you've said, 'yes' ... the people that are actually there [in ICCs] don't have ... the ability to be able to make a call that can be carried through. (O'Flynn et al. 2011: 249–250)

Similar arguments can be mounted about the effects of budget rules on agility and resilience. To take one example, centralization of budget decision-making can impede the agility of policy and operational staff in responding to crises and turbulence, in terms of both managing downside risk and exploiting upside opportunity. Another is where resilience can be impaired by the inability in a particular crisis to shift funds from emergency response to disaster recovery. However, these varied experiences survey only some ways that budget rules can inhibit the conditions necessary for collaboration, agility, or resilience, albeit probably the most important. We now propose to develop a more systematic schema for analyzing the impacts of budget rules on flexibility.

## 3.2 Defining Flexibility in the Budgeting Context

In common usage, according to the *Oxford Dictionary of English* (2010), 'flexibility' refers to an 'ability to be easily modified'. In the expansive organizational studies literature, by way of contrast, the concept of 'flexibility', though contested, usually has a much more specific meaning as a *property of control* (Kickert 1985). In that setting, flexibility can be understood as 'the degree to which an organization possesses a variety of actual and potential procedures, and the rapidity by which it can implement these procedures, in order to increase the control capability of management and improve the controllability of the organization and the environment' (De Leeuw and Volberda 1996: 131). Translating this inexactly into the public budgeting context that we are exploring here, this becomes a matter of how readily budget allocations, expenditures, and reporting processes can be varied to enable useful responses to nonroutine problems. And this in turn is largely a function of how much decision-making authority is *devolved* to those dealing with those problems, in particular, those public servants who are 'close to the coal-face' or involved in collaboration with other organizations.

Based as they are on a rationale of control, budgeting and financial management systems almost mechanically complicate efforts to engage in collaboration. Public sector officials who find themselves in nonroutine situations—the delegates and boundary spanners (Williams 2002)—typically have limited capacity to make authoritative decisions about budget reallocations, which are the domain of officials at higher levels in government. This suggests, therefore, that flexibility in budget processes should be seen as largely a matter of *devolution* of decision-making authority. Unquestionably, at every stage of those processes, someone in effect has the flexibility to assign and reassign monies to nonroutine purposes. The key problem is that across most of those stages, there is considerable distance between that 'someone' and the situation in question, with attenuated information and layers of management separating them from the operational matter. Further complications arise from the fact that the degree of flexibility or devolution may vary across the stages of budgeting.

All of this signposts the need for a multidimensional definition of flexibility. In Table 3.2 we propose two dimensions—levels of budget decision-making and budget rule variability—functioning across the main stages of budgeting. By the *stages* of budgeting we mean the sequence of activities that characterize the formulation, adoption and implementation of budgets within government (Guess and Leloup 2010: 25–30). In a typical Westminster-based parliamentary system—the selected setting for our analysis—this encompasses a calendar of legal and administrative processes for budget preparation by the executive and its approval by the parliament, and the three primary implementation tasks of budget execution: management (converting budgets into operational plans), control (spending approval and checking), and assessment (reviewing budget compliance and program performance). We readily acknowledge these processes are

**Table 3.2** Levels and dimensions of flexibility in budgeting

| | *Budget formulation and adoption* | | *Budget implementation* | | |
|---|---|---|---|---|---|
| | *Budget preparation* | *Budget approval* | *Budget management* | *Budget control* | *Performance assessment* |
| Stages of budgeting | • Budget parameters<br>• Budget decision process<br>• Executive negotiation and decision on allocations | • Budget format<br>• Legislative review and decision<br>• Appropriations | • Allocate resources internally<br>• Implement service plans<br>• Manage finances<br>• Adjust activities and allocations | • Spending authority and budget compliance<br>• Financial reporting<br>• Executive or legislative process for adjustments | • Performance reporting<br>• Periodic evaluations<br>• Ad hoc reviews<br>• Audit |
| Dimensions of variability | • Multiyear fiscal rules, e.g., borrowing constraints, budget planning, tax measures<br>• Annual budget objectives, e.g., surplus or deficit<br>• Budget process design, e.g., individual minister/entity basis, integration of program information | • Budget presentation and review, e.g., allocating to inputs, programs or outcomes, recurrent vs. capital expenditure<br>• Money bills & legislative veto<br>• Relationship between appropriations and budget presentation | • Budget implementation, e.g., allocating within and between inputs, processes, outputs, programs or outcomes<br>• Relationship between appropriations and internal resource allocation | • Budget controls as either approval to spend (e.g., drawing rights) or monitoring, (e.g., reporting and variance analysis)<br>• Focus on budget compliance vs. program performance<br>• Executive or legislative processes for spending or timing adjustments | • Focus on budget compliance vs. program performance<br>• Range of regular and ad hoc evaluation and review<br>• Integration of nonfinancial performance information with budget and management processes |

(*continued*)

**Table 3.2** (continued)

| | | *Budget formulation and adoption* | | *Budget implementation* | | |
|---|---|---|---|---|---|---|
| | | *Budget preparation* | *Budget approval* | *Budget management* | *Budget control* | *Performance assessment* |
| Level of decision-maker | Parliament | ■ | ■ | | ■ | |
| | Prime Minister and/or Finance Minister | ■ | ■ | | ■ | ■ |
| | Portfolio Minister | ■ | ■ | | ■ | ■ |
| | Central Finance Agency | ■ | ■ | ■ | ■ | |
| | Department Head | ■ | | ■ | ■ | ■ |
| | Program Manager | | | ■ | ■ | ■ |
| | Frontline public official | | | | | |

rather stylized, conceived here as distinct and sequential, when in reality they can overlap and/or involve feedback loops.

The first dimension of flexibility is the *level of budget decision-maker*, whose authority is conferred by the law and/or is attached to the office they occupy within an organizational hierarchy. In Table 3.2 we distinguish a number of conventional levels, from high to low in terms of the authority or positional power potentially wielded within the formal processes of budgeting, and we offer no more than a pointer of where each level might be customarily expected to exert influence. It is quite *conceivable* for any level of decision-maker, from frontline officials and program managers to department heads and ministers to have more or less authority to determine budget issues. The greater the number of levels that have budget decision-making authority (which in practice generally means the lower the level of actors to whom power to make decisions is devolved) the more the budget system can be said to be flexible.

The second dimension—which we label budget *rule variability*—is the range of alternative options for each type of budget rule. We will examine the nature and consequences of budget control rules in significantly more detail (see Chap. 4), and in Table 3.2 we set out a range of practices purely to illustrate each budgeting stage. The wider the array of possibilities available to a decision-maker for any given rule, the more flexible that rule is. For instance, in the 'budget management' column of Table 3.2, if managers in all departments are permitted to reallocate funds only within organizational units or within programs, that would be less flexible than were they able to allocate between units or programs.

In summation, flexibility has both 'vertical' and 'horizontal' dimensions. The vertical dimension concerns how far down the hierarchy decision-making authority is devolved (or how far it is decentralized from central to line agencies): the further down (or further out) this authority is extended, the more flexible the system can be said to be. The horizontal dimension covers the degree of latitude within the budget rules for varying decisions about purposes, distributions, reallocations, control, and performance assessment: the more alternative options there are in each rule for managers to select from, the more flexible the system. In this way, flexibility can be conceived as the *product* of the extent of vertical devolution and horizontal variability. A flexible system is one with substantial devolution of decision-making authority to public officials further down the hierarchy (or those operating at a distance from central agencies) and substantial latitude for them to vary their responses to the rules.

## Notes

1. The Oxford Dictionary of English (2010) defines a rule as 'one of a set of explicit or understood regulations or principles governing conduct or procedure within a particular area of activity'.
2. A more finely grained distinction could be made between 'budget rules' (which might apply to the authorization and acquittal of planned expenditures) and 'financial management rules' (which might apply to the system of management practices and accounting information for tracking and reporting expenditures). It is, for example, quite conceivable that interaction between the two categories of rules could, over time, lead to very different outcomes in terms of overall budgetary control and flexibility (such as the constraints that accrual accounting rules are reputed to impose on multiyear budget management, noted later in Chap. 5). However, for ease of exposition, we take the term 'budget rules' to encompass both categories.

## References

ANAO. 2012. *Australian government co-ordination arrangements for indigenous programs.* Audit Report No. 8 2012-13. Canberra: ANAO.

Campbell, D. 2012. Public managers in integrated services collaboratives: What works is workarounds. *Public Administration Review* 72(5): 721–730.

De Leeuw, A.C.J., and H.W. Volberda. 1996. On the concept of flexibility: A dual control perspective. *Omega: The International Journal of Management Science* 24(2): 121–139.

Guess, G.M., and L.T. Leloup. 2010. *Comparative public budgeting: Global perspectives on taxing and spending.* Albany, NY: State University of New York Press.

Halligan, J. 2008. *The Centrelink experiment: Innovations in service delivery.* Canberra: ANU Press.

Jones, L.R., and F. Thompson. 1986. Reform of budget execution control. *Public Budgeting & Finance* 6(1): 33–49.

Kickert, W.J.M. 1985. The magic word flexibility. *International Studies of Management and Organization* XIV(4): 6–31.

McDaid, D. 2012. Joint budgeting: Can it facilitate intersectoral action? In *Intersectoral governance for health in all policies: Structures, actions and experiences,* ed. D. McQueen, M. Wismar, V. Lin, C. Jones, and M. Davies, 111–127. Copenhagen: World Health Organization.

Mitchell, D., and K. Thurmaier. 2011. Toward a theory of budgeting for collaboration. Paper presented at the Public Management Research Conference, Maxwell School of Citizenship and Public Affairs, Syracuse University, NY, 2–4 June 2011.

O'Flynn, J., F. Buick, D. Blackman, and J. Halligan. 2011. You win some, you lose some: Experiments with joined-up government. *International Journal of Public Administration* 34(4): 244–254.

Raine, J., and P. Watt. 2013. Budgetary models, motivation and engagement in financial collaborations. *Public Management Review* 15(6): 878–898.

Raine, J., P. Watt, I. O' Donovan, D. Pritchard, and J. Cattell. 2011. *Integrated public service budgets*. Report of a Research Project for the Local Authorities Research Councils Initiative. March. Birmingham: Institute of Local Government Studies, University of Birmingham.

Ruffner, M., and J. Sevilla. 2004. Public sector modernisation: Modernising accountability and control. *OECD Journal on Budgeting* 4(2): 123–141.

Thompson, F. 1993. Matching responsibilities with tactics: Administrative controls and modern government. *Public Administration Review* 53(4): 303–318.

Williams, P. 2002. The competent boundary spanner. *Public Administration* 80(1): 103–124.

CHAPTER 4

# Budget Rules and Budget Flexibility

**Abstract** This chapter develops a simplified framework for conceptualizing budget control. It surveys the centrality of budgeting to organizational control, and focuses on the traditional model of public budgeting to better understand why its practices remain prevalent in government. The chapter develops a new taxonomy to characterize general 'budget rules' in the public sector and uses two of the most prominent rules (the 'annuality' and 'purpose' of spending) to explain how the rules operate through key properties of control. The chapter explores what high flexibility looks like for each of the budget rules and speculates on the implications for sustainable rule modification.

To explain how the dimensions of flexibility operate in the specific context of public budgeting, we suggest that traditional approaches to budgeting can be characterized by a set of general rules of budget control and that, by way of contrast, its modernized alternative (and especially performance-based budgeting) is essentially rule modification *calculated to increase both control and flexibility* (Cothran 1993).[1] We begin by surveying how budgeting and financial management is conventionally understood in the public sector and how it compares with approaches in the private sector.



M. Di Francesco, J. Alford, *Balancing Control and Flexibility in Public Budgeting*, DOI 10.1007/978-981-10-0341-7_4

## 4.1 An 'Organizational Imperative': Approaches to Analyzing Budgeting

It is almost beyond dispute that in both public and private sectors budgeting is one of the primary functions that enables planning and control in organizations. As both a product and a process, 'the budget' is directed at reconciling spending with constrained revenues (which in the public sector equates principally to sovereign rights to tax and issue debt). While in both contexts budgeting is easily depicted as a purely technical question about the *methods* of financial control, it has long been recognized to be a political question that goes to the resolution of competing priorities and the manner in which conflict and bargaining influence those decisions (which, in government, are structured by the way authority is controlled and accounted for).[2] As a result, theories about budgeting, especially in the public sector, tend to focus on describing and explaining budget formulation (budget decision processes and their documentation, or how allocative decisions are made) and budget execution (budget implementation systems and techniques, or how allocations are managed and controlled) (see Mitchell and Thurmaier 2012: 2). The public budgeting literature is multidisciplinary and vast, and on both counts has its deepest reservoir in the US context, but for our explanatory purposes we will abbreviate this into two general conceptual approaches.[3]

The first approach analyzes the *routines* of budgeting and the way these are shaped by, and help to shape, distinct roles and interactions of institutional actors within government. Such theories are almost synonymous with the concept of 'incrementalism', or the way bounded rationality and conflict management constrict budget decisions to small changes to an existing base of expenditure. Of highest prominence are variations on Aaron Wildavksy's 'guardians and spenders' explanation of how budget routines institutionalize 'rationing' and 'claiming' roles on the basis of specialization and mutual understandings (Wildavsky 1979). Over a lengthy period this literature has been characterized by oscillating arguments around the extent to which fiscal boom and bust, and the regular 'reform' of budget procedures, has actually altered incrementalism as a type of systemic inherency within government (Rubin 1990).

The social choice consequences of budgetary actors engaging in self-interested behavior constitute the second *economic* approach. It is often associated with public choice theories that emphasize the ways utility maximizing behavior by political actors, but especially bureaucrats and sectional interests, can drive budget maximization; it is frequently joined with new institutional economic analysis that views budget maximization as essentially a specification and monitoring problem of 'agency' (Lane 1995). While highly influential in policy terms (Hughes 2003: 10–13), and exemplified perhaps by the contract-based performance reforms underpinning the New Zealand model of public management in the 1980s and 1990s (Boston et al. 1996: 16–40), the economic approach has just as often been critiqued for overplaying the role of self-interest as a motivator and certainly the extent to which formalized monitoring schemes can align interests and improve the rationality of budgeting remains an open question (Anders 2001; Robinson 2000).

Divergent as they are, these two approaches to explaining public budgeting are connected in important ways. They share a focal point that seeks to dispel budgeting in government as a chastely technical exercise, and to expose the intrinsically political nature of resource allocation and its management. And by so doing, both perspectives are actually commentaries on the way that budget routines and roles are sited within broader—and, many might say, monolithic—institutional structures of government accountability. In the political systems we use as the focal point for our analysis—majoritarian Westminster-type parliamentary systems—constitutional arrangements guarantee that the principle of annual appropriation serves not only as a foundation for the answerability of executive government but is also, through 'confidence and supply', the very basis for government formation (Rhodes et al. 2009). Since the late 1600s, these systems evolved to accord parliament supreme constitutional power to approve the funds available to government and the purposes for which they can be expended.[4] The main mechanism of parliamentary control was a cash-based system of government accounting that operated in conjunction with consolidated 'fund' accounts (Funnell et al. 2012). The almost ritualistic role of the annual budget has determined that government accountability has traditionally worked through the *control locus* of ministerial departments and a *performance focus* on legal compliance and financial inputs.

However, the role of politics is not confined to budgeting in the public sector. An informative exercise is briefly to compare these norms and practices with orthodox budget practice in the private sector. Much is made of the dissimilarities in context—most obviously the competitive discipline of markets and the relative precision of profit as a yardstick—and the wellspring of innovation that this is said to represent for organizational structures and managerial practices (Dittenhofer 2001). By and large, however, budgeting in the private sector continues to be informed by two longstanding models: traditional management control systems and responsibility budgeting (Otley 1999; cf. Jones and Thompson 2000). The former rests on a 'command and control' orientation that assigns annually determined targets to functional accountabilities; the latter is a common form of 'remote control' budgeting by a strategic apex in still prevalent multidivisional organizational structures.

Much like their public budgeting equivalents, both forms of corporate budgeting are in essence hierarchical, and neither is safe from accusations of acting as a drag on organizational performance. Indeed, contemporary approaches to budget reform in the private sector have converged on versions of the 'performance trap', or the way annual fixed budget targets distort a manager's capacity to respond flexibly to altering circumstances (see, for example, Hope and Fraser 2003; Otley 2006; Frow et al. 2010; cf. Merchant 1985). The different threads of this literature also point to key modes of solution, some of which are quite conservative and correspond with the modernization agenda pursued in government—like relocating budget decision-making authority to operating managers—and others which are decidedly more drastic—such as replacing preset budget targets with continuously updated performance criteria (the notion of 'relative performance contracts'). All of this counsels that even though in the private sector budget targets remain an 'organizational imperative' for cost control and financial performance, it is also readily conceded that they blunt the incentives for and scope of managerial agility (Otley 1999).

## 4.2 Developing a Basic Taxonomy of Budget Rules

> Every criticism of traditional budgeting is undoubtedly correct ... Why, then, has traditional budgeting lasted so long? Because it has the virtue of its defects ... it is simpler, easier, more controllable, more flexible than modern alternatives. (Wildavsky 1978: 508)

Thus far, our discussion of budgeting has focussed on the underlying rationale of control and the way that defining characteristics of traditional accountability in government can frame budgetary behavior in certain ways. If Aaron Wildavsky (epigraph, above) was broadly right about *why* the traditional budget endures—and the premise for this book is that it *does*—then it ought to be possible to characterize the simplicity of its design as a set of interlocking control mechanisms. In this section we approach this task in two ways. First, we will propose a set of 'general rules of budget control' that depict traditional budgeting in government and, second, we will describe how these rules tend to operate by focusing on the two dimensions of flexibility, introduced earlier. Such an enterprise is inevitably reductionist, but we are resolutely of the view that a basic taxonomy of budget rules is vital both to describing how flexibility is constrained as well as assessing the prospects for its expansion.[5]

We noted earlier that the 'traditional' accountability of government in Westminster-type parliamentary systems is effectively equated with *financial control*. This comprises the formation of government and its answerability to parliament through the twin conventions of 'confidence and supply' and individual ministerial responsibility. The conventions have operated via three standard features of financial control:

- the chain of accountability (the delegation of spending authority and the answerability of delegates to superordinates within organizational hierarchies);
- the concept of fiduciary accountability (the management of public monies is accounted for principally, if not exclusively, through regularity and legality); and
- the financial objective of economy (expenditure control is wielded through fixed financial inputs) (Funnell et al. 2012: 42–64).

Against this background, it does us well to remember that it is only relatively recently—since the late 1970s or so—that fiduciary accountability in government has been expanded to encompass control and accountability in relation to measurable efficiency and effectiveness of service delivery.

These traditional controls can also be distinguished by type and purpose (Jones and Thompson 1986; Thompson 1993; Tommasi 2013). Ex ante controls are applied before spending occurs; they take the form of legal requirements or regulations enforced by budget controllers about what may or may not take place in a budget (for example, approval of payments prior to commitment). Ex post controls, on the other hand, are applied during or after spending occurs; they take the form chiefly of post-implementation scrutiny (for instance, through financial reporting and external audit). In government, financial accountability and control has been weighted heavily toward ex ante controls, and the modus operandi of budget modernization under the new public financial management has been the movement toward ex post controls.

In essence, budget control within traditional public financial administration is dominated by an imperative to 'avoid (control) budget deviations' (Johansson and Siverbo 2014: 273). We contend that this prime directive of traditional budget control can be synthesized into a small number of 'general rules'. In Table 4.1 we describe six discrete rules with the aim of specifying basic properties of budget control. These rules, and their corresponding control properties, are concerned with:

1. who can spend (accountability);
2. how much can be spent (amount);
3. what it can be spent on (purpose);
4. when it must be spent (time);
5. how spending can be changed (transfers); and
6. how spending is accounted for (information).

The operation of the rules can be explained by the way they limit discretion—or delegated authority—and how they do so in combination with other rules. We believe that these rules are pervasive, in fact so deeply ingrained are they in political and administrative institutions that irrespective of efforts at rule change they are quite simply taken for granted by participants as ways of seeing and doing.

We concede the exercise is artificial—arguably some of the 'rules' are indistinguishable—but separating out properties permits us to examine the way they are ***designed*** to interact, which we contend is equally important in explaining their staying power. The rules have diverse provenance and can take different forms: some are enshrined in constitutional instruments, others reside in statute law and administrative regulations, and others still function largely through institutional norms and shared understandings. In addition, while their specific application varies between administrative systems, the rules represent common practices that, irrespective of the type of rule change that has marked efforts at modernization, appear to have ***enduring influence*** on important features of financial management if not broader administrative behavior. This is the simplicity of form and function that Wildavsky admires.

To illustrate, consider the accountability rule governing 'who can spend'. It plainly corresponds with the elementary need to identify a 'budget holder'

**Table 4.1** General rules of budget control

| *Rule* | *Description* | *Examples* | *Impact on discretion* |
|---|---|---|---|
| 1. Accountability | Who can spend | • Parliamentary appropriations to departments or ministers<br>• Legislation sets out financial accountability of department head<br>• Departmental delegations specify staff positions authorized to spend | • Political accountability rests with minister<br>• Departmental head has legal responsibility for department appropriation<br>• Spending authority matched to seniority rather than proximity to program |
| 2. Amount | How much can be spent | • Parliamentary appropriations specify total amounts for expenditure<br>• Program structures specify budget allocation amounts<br>• Department delegations nominate upper limits on authority to spend | • Program structure is explanatory and amounts can be changed (but see 6)<br>• Program structures may not correspond with management structures<br>• Spending authority may not correspond with program allocations |
| 3. Purpose | What it can be spent on | • Parliamentary appropriation specifies a purpose<br>• Program structures categorize budget allocations on the basis of objectives, inputs, activities or outputs<br>• Department delegations nominate operational areas of responsibility in which spending can be incurred | • Program structure is defined by departments and can be changed<br>• Program structures may not correspond with management structures<br>• Spending authority may not correspond with program management |
| 4. Time | When it must be spent | • Parliamentary appropriations authorize spending for a discrete time period, usually one financial year (annuality) | • Prevailing emphasis on managing spend to annual limit<br>• Restricts ability to bring planned expenditure forward or to carryover unused expenditure to subsequent years |

*(continued)*

**Table 4.1** (continued)

| *Rule* | *Description* | *Examples* | *Impact on discretion* |
|---|---|---|---|
| 5. Transfers | How spending can be changed | • Most amounts cannot be reallocated between categories of appropriations, e.g., between purposes or between departments (virement)<br>• Some amounts do not lapse at year end and are available to be spent in subsequent years, e.g., departmental operating costs | • Restricts ability to reallocate amounts between purposes and between departments without central agency or parliamentary approval<br>• Ability to carryover unused operating costs but restricted by central approval processes |
| 6. Information | How spending is accounted for | • Monthly financial reporting to monitor the use of cash and to track the budget against revised current year estimates<br>• Annual reporting of previous years' financial results and comparison of actual versus planned nonfinancial performance set out in budget statements | • Prevailing emphasis on managing spend to annual limit<br>• Budget performance is reported and assessed on a year-to-year basis<br>• In-year reporting focus is on financial rather than nonfinancial performance |

for accountability purposes, whether a political budget holder (such as through an appropriation to a minister of state) or a managerial budget holder (usually the statutory financial administration duties of a departmental head or equivalent). It is, of course, axiomatic in bureaucracy, public or private, that the authority to spend is in turn delegated to prescribed staffing positions—ordinarily matched to seniority rather than proximity to where or what the funds are budgeted for—and that the 'who can spend' rule operates in close combination with other rules covering amount, purpose, and transfers (for the classic treatment, see Foldes 1955). In the specific context of the accountability rule, therefore, there are two defining issues with which budget modernization has been preoccupied: first, the way an apex 'budget holder' must ultimately be accountable for expenditure and, second, the deadening effects of highly prescriptive cascading budget delegation. In short, how best to match budget responsibility with spending authority is the grist to this mill. Similar analysis can be conducted for each of the remaining rules set out in Table 4.1. However, for the purposes of brief exposition, we will confine our attention to two rules that have especially prominent status in defining financial control in the public sector: when funds must be spent (the timeframe of spending) and what funds can be spent on (the purpose of spending).

## 4.3 Exemplar 1: The 'Time' Rule

The first of these rules corresponds with the *principle of annuality* which, as periodic authorization to tax and spend, is of course the central concept of parliamentary control of the executive. Practically all governments in the world have annual budget cycles, which has quite profound and well-known impacts on financial management. In essence, annuality requires budget allocations to be spent during a discrete time period, usually a financial (as opposed to a calendar) year. There is a tallying of spending against the budget—application of the 'how much can be spent' (amount) rule—and both underspending and overspending have consequences. The former means any remaining funds are lost to the budget holder, which can encourage expenditure surge (the annual phenomenon of departments desperately trying to spend money in the last month or two of the financial year) (Forster 1990).[6] The latter is usually seen as a more serious matter, and in many regimes can attract penalties for either the individual budget holder or the organizational unit, or both. In fact, the 'time' rule has been characterized as perhaps *the* source of inflexibility in public budgeting because it embodies a type of 'double-bind': annuality creates demands on a budget holder *simultaneously* to avoid overspending (at the risk of illegality) and underspending (at the risk of losing unused funding from a budget) (Hyndman et al. 2007: 217). The more strictly annuality is enforced, the more likely management behavior aligns itself to compliance with fixed budgets.

It should be no surprise then that the annuality factor of the 'time' rule has been a primary target of budget modernization strategies. At its height in the 1980s and 1990s, the new public financial management not only encouraged a relaxation of budget control rules but in particular placed a premium on expanding the time horizon for financial management to enable greater funding certainty and managerial freedom (Olson et al. 1998). This is perhaps best illustrated by the coupling of multiyear planning frameworks for the annual budget cycle with a loosening of the annuality restrictions on some budget authorizations, normally operating expenses.[7] The key discretionary changes, illustrated by the pioneering 'running costs' system implemented by the Australian Department of Finance in the 1980s and early 1990s, included the ability to carry forward (limited) unspent balances from one year to the next, more latitude in determining the timing or allotment of funds, and greater optionality to retain within the organizational unit some or all of any savings made (Rothman and Thornton 1990; Keating and Holmes 1990). The expectation, of course, was that this type of rule change would not only increase flexibility and rationality—something that proponents argued could ultimately be measured by declines in year-end expenditure surge—but also relieve some of the 'double-bind' attitudinal pressure that annuality imposes on budget managers.

It is curious that, for a rule change of such magnitude, the relaxation of annuality in budget control has rarely been investigated.[8] The evidence that is available, however, suggests that year-end flexibility has had at best marginal impact on the influence of the 'time' rule. An illustrative example is the introduction of carry forward rules for unspent balances as part of the implementation of resource (accrual) accounting in the UK central government (Hyndman et al. 2007). In this case, while HM Treasury and spending departments came to an understanding on the operation of carryovers at the sectoral level, the new arrangements were *not* replicated for lower level budget holders *within* departments. Not only did officials working within departments tend to accept the need for annuality, they were generally highly supportive of it, with departmental financial controllers in particular acknowledging that annuality helped to manage 'risks' relating to overspending and underspending. Those risks were more often than not political: departmental officials felt pressure to *avoid* carryovers rather than have their minister 'explain a surplus'. In other words, the 'time' rule remained timeless:

> annuality still dominates front-line managers' thinking and actions ... good intention has run up against cultural, institutional and political barriers that appear to accept (and, in some cases, value) the structures of tight annual controls. (Hyndman et al. 2007: 234–235)

## 4.4 Exemplar 2: The 'Purpose' Rule

Defining status can also be ascribed to the second rule of budget control, *purpose*, or what it is that funds can be spent on. Like periodicity, highly prescriptive purposes for spending have been an indispensable ingredient for parliamentary control of the executive. This has operated predominantly through two mechanisms. The first, and most heavily condemned, is the traditional form of line-item expenditure budgeting in which legislative purpose equates to the inputs to administration—salaries, material, and equipment—almost without exception on an organizational basis. Purpose, in other words, was simply input to activity. The second, related device was that line-item budget authorizations often operated at the highest legal level—parliamentary appropriations—requiring laborious approval processes to amend items or to transfer funding between lines. Combined, these control mechanisms are virtually indistinguishable from the transfer rule (how spending can be changed) or what in the public administration literature is more commonly referred to as 'virement' (Schiavo-Campo and McFerson 2008: 169).

Transformation of the purpose rule has an even longer lineage than the new public financial management driven changes to annuality, in substance dating back to at least the 'programming planning budgeting' (PBB) systems pioneered by the US Department of Defense in the early 1960s (for the definitive analysis see Schick 1966). We now take for granted that government budgets are organized as some variation of a program structure, where appropriations are categorized either as activities supporting a shared objective, as discrete outputs, or even with regard to the outcomes that an organization plans to achieve. Put another way, purpose is reconfigured in relation to *objectives* and what is produced. The advantages of such a program budget are quite familiar: programs help to clarify the objectives of government action, provide clearer description of the outputs produced, and combine line-item expenditures on the basis of total program cost (Robinson and van Eden 2007). Such features are intended to permit decision-makers to compare qualitatively different activities and, importantly for our discussion, give program managers greater latitude in the choice of inputs to deliver specified program outputs. In sum, the wider the program scope and the more aggregated the budget line authorization, the more flexibility program managers have in modifying purposes and transferring funds between them.

This modernization of the purpose rule is emblematic of the shift from ex ante to ex post budget control under new public financial management. The budget 'program' is widely regarded as the core organizing concept that links budgeting and operational management within a contemporary performance management control system, whereby the program is the level at which a manager is assigned *both* increased budget authority and flexibility (Robinson 2007). A good example is the complex 'output' architecture used in the New Zealand state sector reforms of the 1980s and 1990s: through detailed specification of the goods and services to be 'purchased' by government, these reforms aimed to decentralize budgetary control through contract-based performance accountabilities for organizations and their senior executives (Pallot 1991: 170–173; Boston et al. 1996: 264–279). However, this particular property of budget control is also afflicted by various internal contradictions, which are themselves a product of the interaction between the purpose rule and the 'transfer' rule that restricts movement of funds between appropriations. Three such inconsistencies come readily to mind.

The first of these is that any program structure creates standardized budget categories—'boxes' for money—that are potentially as contrived and obstructive as any expenditure classification based on line items, functions or organizations. Both departments and program managers are, therefore, likely to be inclined to define programs in highly aggregated terms. A second, related problem is that the institutional settings of accountability mean that the legislature and executive have very different strategic interests in the operation of the transfer rule, so that the appropriate level of *disaggregation* for program structures emerges as the key mechanism for regulating managerial flexibility (Bourdeaux 2008).[9] Since program definition is more an art than science—a program can be specified along any number of product or organizational lines—this is, as we have seen, as much a political question as a technical issue. Third, the malleability of program specification tends to undermine its claim to increase executive control through standardization. The program 'concept', which is reliant on increasingly detailed activity description at subprogram levels, can also be understood as a bureaucratic 'technology' that enables program managers to institutionalize and defend their own sectional interests through notionally 'rational' means (Olson 1990). On this interpretation, the 'certainty' delivered by budget program structures is little more than a veneer for legitimizing competing interests within an organization.

## 4.5 Budget Rule Variability: What High Flexibility Might Look Like

The 'time' and 'purpose' rules underscore how traditional public financial accountability works through distinct control properties. They are certainly only representative of the 'general rules' we have proposed, but their investigation helps to explain how such rules have over time been designed—or perhaps accepted as 'tried and tested'—to limit different aspects of budgetary discretion and to operate in combination so as to be mutually reinforcing. The time and purpose rules, in particular, point to the prevalence and enduring influence of the general rules in contemporary budget and administrative practice.

However, we have also suggested that within government organizations, flexibility can be conceived as operating along two dimensions: a vertical aspect corresponding to devolution and a horizontal aspect gauged by the discretion that decision-makers have to vary rules. Accepting that the general budget rules *appear* to be firmly entrenched in administrative attitudes and behavior, we now examine what *scope* exists for rule variability as a source of flexibility. To put this another way, what might high flexibility look like for each rule; how would this compare with the imputed low flexibility of traditional budgeting; and what are the key implications for rule modification? We stress that in this exercise the concepts of 'low' or 'high' flexibility should not necessarily be seen in normative terms but rather as constructs to support analysis of administrative practice.

In Table 4.2 we present a spectrum analysis of budget rule variability by setting out situations that could conceivably characterize low and high flexibility. To enable this we have adjusted our treatment of individual control properties for the general rules in two ways: first, to more clearly account for the vertical dimension of flexibility, we have devised an analytically separate rule category of 'delegated authority' that distinguishes delegation from individual apex accountability; second, to permit a more comprehensive consideration of time period flexibility we have combined the time and amount rule categories. To avoid duplicating too much of the preceding analysis of the general rules, we will concentrate on the conditions typifying 'high flexibility'.

As noted earlier, *individual accountability* for the execution of budget authority has traditionally resided with the most senior office holder, such as a minister of state or a department head. An illustrative example is the longstanding position of 'accounting officer' in the UK central government—usually the permanent secretary of a department—who has a direct accountability to the parliament for the spending and governance of all public money by entities under his or her supervision (Harris 2013). In low flexibility terms, hierarchic accountability dictates that a single—apex—individual is ultimately accountable for the use of budget authority that is usually attached to a single organization (or, increasingly, a 'portfolio' entity that oversights others). In contrast, high flexibility for this rule category could see budget authority attach to the achievement of a broadly defined purpose—or outcome—rather than control and accountability allocated on organizational lines. In this case, accountable officers might have ***multiple budget accountabilities*** for different purposes that could conceivably range across more than one organization. There is, in other words, a 'one-to-many' budget accountability relationship with organizations. These arrangements would be a radical departure from current practice: the closest examples are probably whole-of-government performance frameworks that purport to appropriate funds to 'shared' outcomes but which, in practice, have resembled the 'pooled budget' model within a lead organization's program structure (for example, the Australian 'outcomes and outputs' budget framework, discussed in the next chapter) (MAC 2004: 74–88).

We have also established that in the public sector such budget authority tends to be delegated according to the principle of hierarchy, that is, some combination of seniority and functional authority within an organizational setting. For instance, in the case of UK 'accounting officers', the *operational* responsibility for overall budget control is delegated to the chief finance officer and senior functional executives on the departmental board. This ***delegated authority*** is often prescribed by strict spending limits that are defined with regard to time, amount and permissible fund movement (rules 3 and 5 in Table 4.2). Under a high flexibility scenario, budget authority is not removed altogether from hierarchy but is delegated according to the principle of *subsidiarity*, or the lowest level of an organization that is best able to make a decision. Of course this is not a revelation in organizational design terms, after all program structures were in principle intended to more closely match budget authority with program responsibility. But given that programs—broadly defined—can themselves be a source of rigidity, subsidiarity in this context calls for something rather different. In this set-up there could, for example, be a role for more *situationally determined* spending limits. It would not be unthinkable to decentralize decision rights to take account of different

**Table 4.2** Rule variability and flexibility

| *Rule* | *Description* | *Low flexibility* | *High flexibility* |
|---|---|---|---|
| 1. Accountability (Individual) | Accountability for budget authority resides with an individual (the 'accountable officer') | • A single individual is ultimately accountable for the use of budget authority, i.e., minister or department head<br>• Often one-to-one relationship with an organization (interaction with Rule 4) | • Budget authority relates to a broadly defined purpose (or outcome) so that accountable officers may have multiple accountabilities for different purposes and across different organizations<br>• One-to-many relationship with organizations |
| 2. Delegated authority | Delegation of budget authority within an organization is defined by strict limits | • Budget authority is delegated according to the principle of hierarchy (seniority and functional authority in an organization) and defined by strict spending limits (interaction with Rules 3 and 5) | • Budget authority is delegated according to the principle of subsidiarity (lowest level of organization best able to make decision) and defined by situationally determined spending limits |
| 3. Time and amount limits (Annuality) | Budget authority is granted for a discrete time period (financial year) and places strict limits on the amount and purpose of spending | • Budget authority is limited to one year<br>• Unused allocations must be returned to the center and overspending is sanctioned (interaction with Rules 4 and 5)<br>• Spending must correspond with closely defined legislative purposes | • Budget authority does not lapse, i.e., corresponds with a multiyear period<br>• Budget allocations are retained and continuously adjusted over the multiyear period<br>• Legislated purposes defined in highly aggregated terms |
| 4. Purpose (Budget categories) | Budget authority is classified in terms of defined categories of expenditure, including combinations of organization, inputs, functions or programs | • Budget authority is attached to a single organization (and corresponding accountable officer) (interaction with Rule 1)<br>• Legislative purpose corresponds with highly detailed line items (inputs and/or functions) | • Budget authority is attached to a broadly defined purpose (or outcome) and not a single organization<br>• Legislative purpose and budget planning corresponds with highly aggregated line items (programs or outcomes) |

(*continued*)

**Table 4.2** (continued)

| *Rule* | *Description* | *Low flexibility* | *High flexibility* |
|---|---|---|---|
| 5. Transfer limits (Virement) | Budget authority places limits on transferring funds between budget categories and/or organizations during budget execution | • The reallocation of funds between organizations, or between detailed line items (inputs, functions or programs), is either prohibited or requires ex ante central executive and/or legislative approval (interaction with Rules 3 and 4) | • The reallocation of funds between organizations, or between highly aggregated line items (programs or outcomes), is a process of continuous adjustment determined at the most appropriate organizational level |
| 6. Information requirements | Budget authority specifies performance standards and reporting requirements to enable central oversight during budget execution | • Performance standards are defined in narrow financial terms, i.e., strict compliance with detailed expenditure line items<br>• Reporting requirements are general, frequent, detailed and subject to sanction | • Performance standards are defined in broad terms that integrate financial and nonfinancial, i.e., use of funds to achieve outcomes<br>• Reporting requirements are situational (frequency and content variable) and designed to inform dialogue |

'domains' of discretion, such as the way objectives, managerial seniority, functional responsibility, and proximity to services intersect (Caza 2012; cf. Aubert and Bourdeau 2012).

*Annuality* requires no reintroduction. The high flexibility situation is one where budget authority corresponds with a multiyear period. Again, this is not a novel proposition: as we cover in the next chapter, multi-year planning horizons for budgeting—what are collectively referred to as 'medium term expenditure frameworks'—are a staple of public financial management modernization strategies, even though experience with these has been weighted toward indicative rather than binding expenditure limits, such that in actuality there is only limited certainty in funding allocations (Harris et al. 2013: 143–145). But in a high flexibility budgeting world, funding certainty would permit allocations to be retained and continuously adjusted over the multiyear period. The trade-off, which legislatures are inclined to weigh up very carefully, would be the corresponding need for legislated purposes to be defined in highly aggregated terms.[10] One sustained experience with an adulterated version of multiyear budget planning was the Comprehensive Spending Review (CSR) process used in the UK between the late 1990s and mid-2000s. The CSR process introduced three-year budget allocations that were—in principle—renegotiated every two years based on a review of functional performance as set out in detailed Public Service Agreements (PSAs). However, in practice there were tenuous links between the PSAs and funding levels and, more to the point, budgets continued to be *appropriated* on an annual basis (Smith 2007: 228–231).

*Budget categories*, what we have also called the purpose of spending, captures the way budget authority is controlled by classifications of expenditure, including various combinations of organizational, input-based, functional or programmatic criteria. Budget authority is routinely attached to a single organization—and hence an accountable officer—and in a low flexibility context legislative purpose matches highly detailed line items, between which the movement of funds is proscribed during budget execution (what we have referred to as *transfer limits*). As we have seen, the level of disaggregation associated with budget categories is the focal point for both legislature oversight and executive flexibility: the more highly aggregated budget classifications are, the less control a legislature has and the more flexibility public managers have to reallocate funds between budget categories and/or organizations. This holds for both parliamentary and presidential systems of government, but may be more pronounced in the latter (in the context of the US federal budget process, see Robbins 2005).

In the case of budget categories in a high flexibility setting, therefore, authority is attached to a broadly defined purpose or outcome, highly aggregated line items (ideally a single line) and a virement regime that is effectively a process of continuous adjustment determined at the most appropriate level in relevant organizations (cf. Alesani 2012). As is the case now, 'program' allocations might be either intra-organizational or multiorganizational; however, such allocations could also be *in any one of a range of available budget categories that are apposite to the type of service*. For instance, whereas spending on employment programs might be most usefully oriented to outcomes (such as numbers of clients in jobs for more than six months) this would be more difficult to apply to services for psychiatric patients, where outcomes (for example, numbers of clients with improved psychiatric health) are harder to define, operationalize, and observe, and where it might be more manageable to pay for inputs such as person-days of quality-assured specialist experts. In other words, a high flexibility program structure would permit both 'differentiation' and 'selectivity' in the program structures. An interesting example comes from the Netherlands, where in the late 2000s the province of Groningen introduced a performance budget structure to address councilor concerns about the usability of financial and nonfinancial information attached to standardized programs (Ter Bogt et al. 2015). The modified program structure incorporated 'task variety' in the criteria used to guide program specification: ongoing routine activities (such as refuse collection) require concise, concrete specification as activities and measures, whereas complex activities that must be undertaken collaboratively and which extend over more than one year (such as coordination of housing services) require significantly more elaborated specification as proximate outcomes and indicators (Ter Bogt et al. 2015: 291–296, 305–308).

Lastly, budget execution in both low and high flexibility environments demands *information* to permit governments to ascertain whether its purposes are being met and with what degree of efficiency, effectiveness, equity, or whatever other value it sees as important. This requires budget authority to specify performance standards and reporting requirements. In a low flexibility world, performance standards are defined with regard to financial regularity, in effect strict compliance with expenditure line items. In this context, reporting requirements are typically universal, frequent and highly detailed, and noncompliance is subject to sanction. In a high flexibility environment, performance standards could be defined in broader terms that integrate financial and nonfinancial criteria, that is, how well funds have been used to achieve measurable outcomes. Under these arrangements, reporting requirements become contingency based, meaning the frequency and content of reporting is customized to organizational and programmatic circumstances and designed less with sanction in mind than rewarding functional behavior and encouraging program improvement. It should come as no surprise that this financial management orientation is usually accompanied by an organizational culture of 'evaluation' that places value on integrated review processes (Gray and Jenkins 1993). To a significant extent, the integration of financial and nonfinancial performance and the customization of reporting obligations, especially for external accountability, have been the foci of budget modernization, although they have in practice tended to move in opposite directions: the former has arguably become something of a 'box-ticking' exercise rather than a genuine change in managerial orientation, and the latter has been blunted by the shift toward greater regularization through international standards, such as for general purpose financial reporting (Bandy 2015: 300–306).

This depiction of budget rule variability points to a characterization of high flexibility budgeting as fewer rules, expanded discretion, and lower level decision-making, which of course critics would also portray as a world of profligacy, unaccountability, and, potentially, corruption. This may suggest that reducing the number of rules is not necessarily the answer to the question of how budgeting and financial management practices 'embed' rigidity in administrative practice. Instead, an alternative perspective on budget flexibility may be to *reshape the type of rules and the way they are applied*, rather than move almost instinctively toward fewer rules. Such an approach would give more attention to the 'organizational effectiveness' of budget rules, with the aim of better balancing the technical feasibility of their design and operation with their acceptance by regulators and regulatees alike (as proposed, for instance, in the promising notion of 'green tape') (DeHart-Davis 2009; DeHart-Davis et al. 2013). The merits of the shift toward 'rule-shaping'—rather than simply 'rule-shaving'—is a theme we return to in Chap. 6.

## Notes

1. Or to put this another way, modernized public budgeting uses 'third order controls' to more effectively leverage the familiar 'bureaucratic paradox' that an efficient organization is one that must centralize in order to decentralize (Perrow 1977). This point will receive more treatment in Chap. 6.
2. The classic formulation of the key budgeting question in government is that coined by its namesake, V.O. Key, 'On what basis shall it be decided to allocate x dollars to activity A instead of B?' (Key 1940: 1138).
3. Budgeting research is multidisciplinary in that its key phenomena have been of interest in disciplines as diverse as economics, political science, public administration, organization studies, psychology, management, and accounting. We concede our characterization of the literature is reductive and inclined toward political science and management, but we note that the two broad approaches we discuss—'routines' and 'economics'—are not inconsistent with other analytical frameworks (for example, Covaleski et al. 2003).

4. Limited in certain of these jurisdictions by the overriding authority of any written constitution, for example as is the case for the Commonwealth (or national) government of Australia.
5. We are not aware of this type of rule taxonomy having been developed specifically in the context of public budgeting. Some have articulated 'classical rules' of budgetary theory, most of which correspond with public finance principles about the relationship between taxation and expenditure (Jones and Pendlebury 2010). Similar taxonomic intentions inform other analyses of budget behavior, such as efforts to classify the incentive effects of budget controls for 'strategic misrepresentation' (Jones and Euske 1991). As we will see, some of these controls—budget constraints, program information asymmetry, detailed and rigid legislative oversight, temporal constraints, and excessive external audit of inputs—have some equivalency in the taxonomy we propose. By and large, though, efforts to develop 'measurement instruments' for budget control are to be found in the private sector context (see, for example, the micro-attributes for 'tight budget control' proposed in Van der Stede 2001).
6. In his discussion, Forster also sets out analysis to demonstrate why expenditure surge can be explained as 'rational behavior' in the sense that perfect 'phasing' of expenditure by public officials is not a realistic strategy for managing risk and uncertainty (Forster 1990: 104–108).
7. Having said this, it is important to recognize that even large components of operating expenses within the public sector are in effect *nondiscretionary*. These include, for instance, eligibility-based statutory entitlements and staffing costs (it is not uncommon for labor costs to account for three-quarters of operating expenses and, whether because of skill set demands or industrial relations arrangements, the related human capital is often not 'fungible').
8. This may be due to the increasing adoption of accrual accounting for budget management in the public sector, which deemphasizes the timing of cash transactions and, in theory at least, obviates the need for carryovers (Lienert and Ljungman 2009).
9. Bourdeaux surveys these issues in the context of sub-national (state) governments operating within the US separation-of-powers system, but the broader observations on the interaction between transfer rules and program definition have no less prescience in other political systems. For a more targeted critique of volatility in the way executive government defines and structures programs and outputs in a Westminster-based parliamentary system, see Carlin (2006).
10. Budgeting as continuous adjustment—where approved spending limits are a starting point for 'rebudgeting' during the reporting period—is certainly not unknown in government but is strongly associated with incrementalism

and informality. For these reasons rebudgeting is often equated with 'repetitive budgeting' (Wildavsky 1986: 17–20), which is seen as an indicator of high levels of institutional incapacity and low levels of budget control.

## References


Alesani, D. 2012. Rethinking budgeting as a continuous process. *Public Administration Review* 72(6): 885–886.

Anders, K.K. 2001. *Beyond results: Accountability, discretion and performance budget reform*. London: JAI Press.

Aubert, B.A., and S. Bourdeau. 2012. Public sector performance and decentralization of decision rights. *Canadian Public Administration* 55(4): 575–598.

Bandy, G. 2015. *Financial management and accountability in the public sector*, 2nd ed. London: Routledge.

Boston, J., J. Martin, J. Pallot, and P. Walsh. 1996. *Public management reform: The New Zealand model*. Auckland: Oxford University Press.

Bourdeaux, C. 2008. The problem with programs: Multiple perspectives on program structures in program-based performance-oriented budgets. *Public Budgeting & Finance* 28(2): 20–47.

Carlin, T. 2006. Victoria's accrual output based budgeting system: Delivering as promised? Some empirical evidence. *Financial Accountability & Management* 22(1): 1–19.

Caza, A. 2012. Typology of the eight domains of discretion in organizations. *Journal of Management Studies* 49(1): 144–177.

Cothran, D.A. 1993. Entrepreneurial budgeting: An emerging reform? *Public Administration Review* 53(5): 445–454.

Covaleski, M.A., J.H. Evans, J.L. Luft, and M.D. Shields. 2003. Budgeting research: Three theoretical perspectives and criteria for selective integration. *Journal of Management Accounting Research* 15: 3–49.

DeHart-Davis, L. 2009. Green tape: A theory of effective organizational rules. *Journal of Public Administration Research and Theory* 19(2): 361–384.

DeHart-Davis, L., J. Chen, and T.D. Little. 2013. Written versus unwritten rules: The role of rule formalization in green tape. *International Public Management Journal* 16(3): 331–356.

Dittenhofer, M.A. 2001. Behavioral aspects of government financial management. *Managerial Auditing Journal* 16(8): 451–457.

Foldes, L. 1955. The delegation of authority to spend. *Economica* 22(87): 246–260.

Forster, J. 1990. Rational managerial behaviour, risk and expenditure surge in the public sector. In *Budgetary management and control: The public sector in Australasia*, ed. J. Forster and J. Wanna, 103–113. Melbourne: Macmillan.

Frow, N., D. Marginson, and S. Ogden. 2010. 'Continuous' budgeting: Reconciling budget flexibility with budgetary control. *Accounting, Organizations and Society* 35(4): 444–461.

Funnell, W., K. Cooper, and J. Lee. 2012. *Public sector accounting and accountability in Australia*, 2nd ed. Sydney: UNSW Press.

Gray, A., and B. Jenkins. 1993. Horses to water: Budgeting, auditing and evaluation in seven governments. In *Budgeting, auditing and evaluation: functions and integration in seven governments*, ed. A. Gray, B. Jenkins, and B. Segsworth, 185–208. New Brunswick, NJ: Transaction.

Harris, J. 2013. *Following the pound: The accounting officer in central government*. London: Institute for Government.

Harris, J., R. Hughes, G. Ljungman, and C. Sateriale. 2013. Medium-term budget frameworks in advanced economies: Objectives, design and performance. In *Public financial management and its emerging architecture*, ed. M. Cangiano, T. Curristine, and M. Lazare, 137–174. Washington, DC: International Monetary Fund.

Hope, J., and R. Fraser. 2003. *Beyond budgeting: How managers can break free from the annual performance trap*. Cambridge: Harvard Business School Publishing.

Hughes, O.E. 2003. *Public management and administration: An introduction*, 3rd ed. London: Palgrave Macmillan.

Hyndman, N., R. Jones, and M. Pendlebury. 2007. An exploratory study of annuality in the UK public sector: plus ca change, plus c'est la meme chose? *Financial Accountability & Management* 23(2): 215–237.

Johansson, T., and S. Siverbo. 2014. The appropriateness of tight budget control in public sector organizations facing budget turbulence. *Management Accounting Research* 25(4): 271–283.

Jones, L.R., and K.J. Euske. 1991. Strategic misrepresentation in budgeting. *Journal of Public Administration Research and Theory* 1(4): 437–460.

Jones, R., and M. Pendlebury. 2010. *Public sector accounting*, 6th ed. Harlow: Pearson.

Jones, L.R., and F. Thompson. 1986. Reform of budget execution control. *Public Budgeting and Finance* 6(1): 33–49.

Jones, L.R., and F. Thompson. 2000. Responsibility budgeting and accounting. *International Public Management Journal* 3(2): 205–227.

Keating, M., and M. Holmes. 1990. Australia's budgetary and financial management reforms. *Governance* 3(2): 168–185.

Key, V.O. 1940. The lack of a budgetary theory. *The American Political Science Review* 34: 1137–1144.

Lane, J-E. 1995. *The public sector: Concepts, models and approaches*. London: Sage.

Lienert, I., and G. Ljungman. 2009. *Carry-over of budget authority*. Fiscal Affairs Department Public Financial Management Technical Guidance Note. Washington, DC: International Monetary Fund.

MAC (Management Advisory Committee). 2004. *Connecting government: Whole of government responses to Australia's priority challenges*. Canberra: MAC.

Merchant, K.A. 1985. Organizational controls and discretionary program decision making: A field study. *Accounting, Organizations and Society* 10(1): 67–85.

Mitchell, D., and K. Thurmaier. 2012. *Currents and undercurrents in budgeting theory: Exploring the swirls, heading upstream*. Public Administration Review Foundations of Public Administration Series. Washington, DC: American Society for Public Administration.

Olson, O. 1990. Qualities of the programme concept in municipal budgeting. *Scandinavian Journal of Management* 6(1): 13–29.

Olson, O., J. Guthrie, and C. Humphrey (eds.). 1998. *Global warning! debating international developments in new public financial management*. Oslo: Cappelen Akademisk Forlag.

Otley, D. 1999. Performance management: A framework for management control systems research. *Management Accounting Research* 10(4): 363–382.

Otley, D. 2006. Trends in budgetary control and responsibility accounting. In *Contemporary issues in management accounting*, ed. A. Bhimani, 291–307. Oxford: Oxford University Press.

Pallot, J. 1991. Financial management reform. In *Reshaping the state: New Zealand's bureaucratic revolution*, ed. J. Boston, J. Martin, J. Pallot, and P. Walsh, 166–197. Auckland: Oxford University Press.

Perrow, C. 1977. The bureaucratic paradox: The efficient organization centralizes in order to decentralize. *Organizational Dynamics* 5(4): 3–14.

Rhodes, R., J. Wanna, and P. Weller. 2009. *Comparing Westminster*. Oxford: Oxford University Press.

Robbins, D. 2005. Administrative discretion: Its use in budgetary analysis. *Public Administration Quarterly* 29(2): 186–200.

Robinson, M. 2000. Contract budgeting. *Public Administration* 78(1): 75–90.

Robinson, M. 2007. Performance budgeting models and mechanisms. In *Performance budgeting: Linking funding and results*, ed. M. Robinson, 1–18. New York: Palgrave Macmillan.

Robinson, M., and H. van Eden. 2007. Program classification. In *Performance budgeting: Linking funding and results*, ed. M. Robinson, 63–87. New York: Palgrave Macmillan.

Rothman, G., and B. Thornton. 1990. Management of budgetary expenditures: The Commonwealth running costs system. In *Budgetary management and control: The public sector in Australasia*, ed. J. Forster and J. Wanna, 92–102. Melbourne: Macmillan.

Rubin, I. 1990. Budget theory and budget practice: How good the fit? *Public Administration Review* 50(2): 179–189.

Schiavo-Campo, S., and H.M. McFerson. 2008. *Public management in global perspective.* New York: M. E. Sharpe.

Schick, A. 1966. The road to PPB: The stages of budget reform. *Public Administration Review* 26(4): 243–258.

Smith, P.C. 2007. Performance budgeting in England: Public service agreements. In *Performance budgeting: Linking funding and results*, ed. M. Robinson, 211–233. New York: Palgrave Macmillan.

Ter Bogt, H., G.J. Van Helden, and B. Van Der Kolk. 2015. Challenging the NPM ideas about performance management: Selectivity and differentiation in outcome-oriented performance budgeting. *Financial Accountability & Management* 31(3): 287–315.

Thompson, F. 1993. Matching responsibilities with tactics: Administrative controls and modern government. *Public Administration Review* 53(4): 303–318.

Tommasi, D. 2013. The budget execution process. In *The international handbook of public financial management*, ed. R. Allen, R. Hemming, and B. Potter, 285–311. New York: Palgrave Macmillan.

Van der Stede, W. 2001. Measuring 'tight budgetary control'. *Management Accounting Research* 12(1): 119–137.

Wildavsky, A. 1978. A budget for all seasons? Why the traditional budget lasts. *Public Administration Review* 38(6): 501–509.

Wildavsky, A. 1979. *The politics of the budgetary process*, 3rd ed. Boston, MA: Little Brown.

Wildavsky, A. 1986. *Budgeting: A comparative theory of budgetary processes.* Revised edition. New Brunswick, NJ: Transaction Publishers.

CHAPTER 5

# Budget Reform and Rule Modification

**Abstract** This chapter illustrates how the trade-offs between control and flexibility are manifested in practice. It surveys the features of NPM-inspired budget modernization in the international context, with a focus on the design intent for 'flexibility' residing within these reform schemes. The chapter integrates the 'budget rule' taxonomy with the dimensions of budget flexibility to analyze the impact of rule interactions in the case of performance-based budget reforms in Australia over the period 1983–2010. Over three phases of restructuring, the chapter identifies four key legacy reforms and shows how the budget rules can be discerned in the design, interaction and redesign of the four reforms.

In this chapter we present a brief case application of our rules framework. The aim is to illustrate the shift from traditional to modernized budget systems in the public sector, and also explain the continuing influence of the general budget rules. We begin by surveying international trajectories in budget modernization to highlight the place of 'flexibility' within the reform agenda for budget systems. We then focus on the experience of an exemplar budget modernizer—Australia—which since the mid-1980s has been acknowledged internationally as a reform leader (Pollitt and Bouckaert 2004: 67–74; Schick 1990). The change agenda pursued by the key bureaucratic actor—the Department of Finance[1]—has often been at the forefront of broader public sector restructuring and has displayed,

 
M. Di Francesco, J. Alford, *Balancing Control and Flexibility in Public Budgeting*, DOI 10.1007/978-981-10-0341-7_5

at the very least, a rhetorical aspiration to our two key dimensions of flexibility, devolution and discretion.[2]

The survey is both chronological, identifying three 'phases' of reform, and stylistic, with the objectives of reviewing milestone institutional and procedural changes and mapping these changes to the general rules of budget control introduced in the previous chapters. We want to demonstrate that a small number of what we call 'legacy' reforms have a reasonable degree of continuity across the reform phases, that the reforms were targeted principally at expanding budget flexibility, but that ultimately the impacts of reform were shaped by the structural and cultural pull of the general rules.

## 5.1 Flexibility and the Trajectory of International Budget Modernization

The advent of NPM in the early-to-mid 1980s ushered in a dramatic shift in the way that governments sought to manage public resources. The shift was relatively swift, sweeping away many of the *forms* of traditional financial administration, and remarkably widespread, with an unprecedented level of *international* adherence by governments. This development was likely attributable to a global process analogous to what organizational theorists call 'institutional isomorphism' (DiMaggio and Powell 1983). In some respects adoption of budget reforms by advanced economies mimicked the better practice 'norms' pioneered by lead countries, and in other respects it operated—at least for a time—as coercion, for example, in the way that international organizations required less developed countries to 'restructure' fiscal institutions as a condition of donor funding (Common 1998).

Our key purpose in this section is scene-setting: we want to contextualize a singular case (budget reform in Australia) within prevailing international trends. In particular, we want to show that a defining feature of this movement has been 'flexibility' in various guises: sometimes in the form of 'deregulation' of procedural control by central finance agencies, other times in the way of 'decentralization' or 'devolution' of spending authority to spending departments, subnational governments or even nongovernment organizations. In asserting this, we do not deny that the new public financial management housed contradictory diagnoses and prescriptions for institutional reform; for example, *centralization* that strengthened top-down spending limits as the bounds for delegating allocative decisions openly jostled with *decentralization* which pursued devolved private sector style financial management as a remedy to the inefficiency of traditional budget controls (Kelly and Wanna 2001; more generally Aucoin 1990). Like the budget rules they sought to mitigate, the one was dependent on the other, and yet both were designed to expand 'flexibility' in distinct ways. There are, we believe, three leading components of international public financial management practices concerned with the decentralization and devolution themes of flexibility as we have defined the term: multiyear planning frameworks, relaxation of input rules, and performance management (OECD 2007). We précis each in turn below.

The first and possibly most pervasive set of reforms are multiyear planning frameworks for budgeting, or what are also known as medium-term expenditure frameworks (MTEFs).[3] In essence, an MTEF integrates the annual budget process with multiyear (usually 3 to 4 year) estimates of revenue and expenditure prepared on a 'no policy change' basis. Its purpose is to account for the fiscal impact of current-year allocation decisions on the forward years (a control issue) and provide a higher degree of funding certainty for spending departments to plan resource management—and potential reallocation—over the multiyear period (a flexibility issue). There are many variations on the theme, but in most MTEFs the forward estimates operate along a continuum ranging from 'indicative' allocations to 'hard' ceilings. In Australia and New Zealand, for example, budget aggregates tend to be indicative with tighter specification of spending allocations at the program level, whereas in leading European reform countries budget estimates are binding at the aggregate level (such as in the Netherlands) or sectoral level (as in France) with more flexibility for reallocation at the ministry and program levels; indeed, in most West European countries where multiyear budgeting is used the approach has been labeled 'Each minister is her own finance minister' (Blondal 2003: 13).

The relaxation of central input controls constitutes the second set of reforms, 'based on the simple premise that the heads of individual agencies are in the best position to choose the most efficient mix of inputs to carry out the agency's activities' (Blondal 2003: 15). Rule modification took a number of forms, some of which we have touched upon in previous chapters: the consolidation of budget lines into a single appropriation for operating expenditures; the decentralization of the personnel management function (on the basis that staffing costs account for the largest category of expenditures); and the redistribution of common services provision (as well as the methods by which these costs are allocated across organizational functions). In addition, in many but certainly not all countries, incentives for more 'entrepreneurial' management were created through 'modern' forms of accrual accounting (to permit more accurate costing of programs, especially the attribution of common services costs) and greater tolerance of carryovers of unexpended funds between years (and hence a concrete way of operationalizing multiyear budget planning) (Rubin and Kelly 2005: 564–567). Each of these changes was a lead indicator of the shift from ex ante to ex post control within the public sector, especially in respect of 'internal financial controls' where devolved management systems have largely replaced centrally located systems for approving payments prior to commitment (Ruffner and Sevilla 2004).

The third group of related reforms is centered on the contribution of budgets to organizational performance, which has broadly been termed a 'focus on results'. The relaxation of input controls and the redistribution of budget authority to lower levels in the administrative system have been advocated in tandem with the introduction of 'performance management control' approaches to public management (Van Dooren et al. 2015: 86–113). Performance-based accountability for public managers is the *quid pro quo* for rule relaxation: funding is categorized on a program basis, programs specify measurable objectives and performance information, and public managers are held accountable for achieving objectives by selecting the most suitable effective mix of resources. Such systems establish institutional capabilities and procedures to specify and monitor performance standards; and, much like the transformation of internal financial controls, accountability is reconfigured as ex post monitoring by central agencies and external auditors of the performance achieved.

## 5.2 The Three Phases of Australian Budget Reform: 1983–2010

### *5.2.1 The Traditional Budget Model (pre-1983)*

Like other Westminster-based parliamentary systems, executive government at the national level in Australia used the 'traditional' model of budgeting and financial administration for the majority of the twentieth century (Groenewegen 1973). Budget decisions were determined centrally by Cabinet—later a subcommittee of senior Ministers—on the advice of the Treasury, the powerful finance and economics ministry.[4] Budget management and control was applied through legal and administrative constraints on the quantum and purpose of spending and labyrinthine approval procedures for transferring funds between lines or organizations. Prepared on a cash basis, budget performance standards were defined in terms of financial regularity and accompanied by frequent, detailed, and sanctionable reporting (Cutt 1983; Weller and Cutt 1976).

For many years the annual budget process featured a habitual 'bid and review' marshaled by the Treasury. Departments submitted 'bids' to the Treasury for new policies or one-off purchases for the new financial year and, if approved 'in principle', departments would develop draft estimates covering both existing activities and Treasury-endorsed new policies that would then be subject to an iterative process of feedback and adjustment. Budget preparation thus progressed often with little or no senior ministerial input until quite late in the process, when Treasury presented Cabinet with revised estimates for review in conjunction with its recommendations for new policies and economic forecasts (Weller and Cutt 1976). Ultimately the Cabinet would establish a budget position and determine each department's expenditure estimates and new spending, but once passed budget execution was a matter of Treasury oversight through preapproval of spending authority in the form of 'drawing rights', and parliamentary scrutiny through detailed regularity auditing by the Auditor-General and review by the standing joint committee on public accounts (Groenewegen 1973).

In the Australian setting, traditional budgeting achieved expenditure control through amount and purpose, permitting budget-holders to incur expenses on inputs that had been predetermined by Cabinet and the Treasury. Budget-holders had authority neither to reallocate funds across input lines or organizations, nor to purchase inputs that were not itemized in the budget. As in comparable jurisdictions, budget authority was confined to the one financial year with no ability either to carry over underspends to subsequent years or bring planned expenditures forward (Weller and Cutt 1976). This system was styled retrospectively by the architects of later budget reform as 'almost exclusively preoccupied with compliance with detailed procedures' (Keating and Holmes 1990: 174).

By the early 1980s a broad consensus had emerged around the need for reform of the Australian public sector, in particular the aspects of traditional budgeting that were obstacles to efficient public administration. Representative of this line of thinking was the Royal Commission on Australian Government Administration (RCAGA) established by the reformist Whitlam Labor Government (1972–1975), which served as a midwife for both 'accountable management' and the integration of strategic planning and evaluation within budget coordination processes. On the former it was an early advocate of budget devolution, arguing that 'managers should be given resources, appropriate authority and expected results, and required to manage these resources accordingly' (RCAGA 1976: 34). On the latter it famously noted that

> The annual budget in its present form is not a suitable instrument for the development of the government's blueprint. It is time-scale limited, and will not be capable of comprehending the longer term implications of the Government's programmes. Its processes do not bring continuing expenditures effectively under review, or provide an adequate opportunity to reassess programmes introduced in circumstances which are now changed or no longer relevant. (RCAGA 1976: 37)

On this rendering, the system entrenched existing allocations of resources, and its inattention to reviewing the relevance of spending made it difficult for governments to implement changed policy priorities and control aggregate expenditure. The lack of flexibility between appropriations and the perverse incentives associated with lapsing annual appropriations were also singled out by spending departments as key inhibitors of effective management, financial or otherwise (Weller and Cutt 1976). And, according to the RCAGA, at the center of this coordination problem was Treasury, an institution that had become 'too privileged, too powerful and too prone to substitute its own judgments, its own values and its own priorities for those of other departments, ministers and the government itself' (RCAGA 1976: 319). This apprehension was formally accepted when the Treasury was split by the Fraser Coalition Government (1975–1983) into separate economic and finance ministries in 1976 (thus creating the current Department of Finance).

### 5.2.2 *The Modernized Budget Model (1983–1999)*

Elected in March 1983, the Hawke Labor Government (1983–1991) is widely considered to be a watershed in systemic budget reform in Australia. The origins, execution, and impact of its change agenda have received extensive treatment elsewhere by both participating practitioners (Holmes and Shand 1995; Keating and Holmes 1990) and scholars (Campbell and Halligan 1992: 124–162; Wanna et al. 2000; Zifcak 1994: 92–133), and suffice for us to note that the modernization agenda in Australia, as elsewhere, was broadly characterized by efforts simultaneously to centralize and decentralize budget control mechanisms (Kelly and Wanna 2001).

The former are evinced in a raft of new budget institutions and procedures designed to strengthen political control of fiscal aggregates. The reinforced role of cabinet budget committees and the application of portfolio budgeting are illustrative examples. The decentralization thrust, which reflected a managerialist view that budget controls impeded efficient financial management, can be observed in the replication of private sector budgeting techniques—most prominently, as discussed in earlier chapters, 'responsibility budgeting', which advocated rationalizing budget lines and devolving budget authority to managers. While NPM has been associated with the joint application of public choice and managerialism, the Australian version, at least during this period, was oriented toward the latter, especially through its emphasis on the benefits of devolution (Campbell and Halligan 1992: 141).

Symbolic of this reform period is the Financial Management Improvement Program (FMIP) which sought initially to 'let the managers manage' by removing highly prescriptive financial controls, and later to 'make the managers manage' by introducing a program management structure that matched expanded decision rights with accountability for measurable results. Devolution—at the time defined carefully as 'the transferral of the *authority and accountability for decisions* away from central agencies to departments and down through levels of department management' (emphasis added, MAB-MIAC 1991: 1)—was based on the widely disseminated management principle that those closest to delivery need latitude to manage program delivery *and* program finances. The aim of the FMIP was, as an influential parliamentary committee at the time put it, 'to free up bureaucratic processes to give public sector managers greater scope and flexibility to manage resources efficiently and effectively' (SCFPA 1990: xi).

In charting the FMIP of the 1980s and early-to-mid 1990s, we spotlight four institutional and procedural modifications that we label 'legacy reforms'. We recognize that they straddle centralizing and decentralizing reform tendencies in this period, but arguably—in both intent and practical effect—they were directed *principally* at expanding the budget flexibility of departments and managers (see also Zifcak 1994: 111–129). We contend these four reforms are a useful vehicle for characterizing this modernization period and illustrating the ongoing influence of the general rules of budget control.

First among these is ***program budgeting*** which supplanted the traditional budget format: switching away from allocating funds to line items, the budget documents appropriated funds to objectives-based 'programs' and, over time, performance indicators. The intention was to transform managerial orientation (and, through redesigned financial reporting to parliament, the accountability concerns of legislators) from inputs and activities to efficiency and effectiveness (Mulgan 2008). Program structures aggregated line items and ostensibly delivered departments, and within them 'program managers', greater scope to fund combinations of inputs that would best achieve program objectives. These changes were complemented by monitoring and review processes, with a special focus on systematized program evaluation (Di Francesco 1998). Significantly, program budgeting was renamed 'program management and budgeting' (PMB) in 1987 to emphasize integrated management as opposed to merely the provision of financial information (MAB-MIAC 1993).

The original FMIP reforms were also marked by the introduction of the ***running costs system*** which consolidated the numerous administrative and operating allocations of each department into a single appropriation (Rothman and Thornton 1990). 'Running costs' typically accounted for around 10 per cent of a department's overall funding. The new arrangements were designed to 'enable' program budgeting and, in addition, permitted departments to carry over a proportion of unused funds into subsequent budget periods—to encourage planning beyond the immediate budget period—and bring forward future funding to meet urgent or high-priority needs where 'resource agreements' had been negotiated with the Department of Finance. The key principle of the running costs system was that managers should have the budget capacity to adapt to changing circumstances (Keating and Holmes 1990: 176–177).

***Portfolio budgeting***, or the devolution of budget decision-making authority from the cabinet to ministers, constitutes the third legacy reform. While it formally commenced in 1985, portfolio budgeting came into its own following the 'landmark' machinery of government changes in 1987 that rationalized departments into expansive cross-functional portfolios (Davis and Craswell 1994). Portfolios were allocated budget envelopes, and ministers handed responsibility both to manage the portfolio expenditure cap and, within total outlay and specific savings targets set by the Expenditure Review Committee (ERC) of Cabinet, to decide program allocations. Portfolio budgeting was the apparatus underpinning Australia's much vaunted 'trade-off' budget system under which a minister desiring to implement a new program would be required to propose offsetting savings from within their own portfolio (Blondal et al. 2008). Although ministers were never given complete discretion about how a portfolio's budget was spent, the system was clearly intended to frame—and reinforce—the benefits expected for departments from PMB and the running costs system (see, for instance, Keating and Holmes 1990: 172–173).

The final legacy reform, the *forward estimates system*, consists of rolling baseline projections of government revenues and expenditures for the three years beyond the budget year on a 'no policy change' basis (that is, existing programs and economic conditions are assumed to be unchanged over the planning period). The estimates were considered the 'core instrument' of the modernized system because they provided a multiyear planning framework integrated with annual budget decision processes—the estimates process tied together strategic policymaking, portfolio budgeting, and internal PMB (Keating and Holmes 1990: 170–172; MAB-MIAC 1993: 230). Treasury had flirted with forward estimates for internal planning processes since the late 1960s (Weller and Cutt 1976), but the real advances in the Australian case were government decisions to publish the estimates (in 1983) and to formally replace the one-year budget estimates (in 1985), both of which commenced the process of reorientating the budget from detailed current-year line items to the outyear funding consequences of ongoing and new programs (Mackay 2011). In summation, significant faith was placed in the forward estimates as a mechanism for delivering greater funding certainty to departments and permitting a more strategic—multiyear, objectives-based and flexible—approach to budgeting.

### 5.2.3 *The Contemporary Budget Model (1999–2010)*

By the middle of the 1990s, the flexibility benefits promised by reforms in the modernization period had not materialized as expected. Despite their devolutionary orientation, there was a perception that the legacy reforms operated within an environment that acquiesced in the continuing management of financial inputs; preserved large swathes of Finance Department supervision; conceded the operation of perverse incentives (including the prevalence of end-of-year expenditure surge); and sent confusing signals by beginning to budget and report on different (cash and accrual) accounting bases (see, for example, Barton 2007; Blondal et al. 2008). Often these assessments were made against a background of unflattering comparisons with the efficiency of financial practices in private corporations.

The arrival of the Howard Coalition Government (1996–2007) in March 1996 heralded a second phase of reform that, while building on the managerialist credentials of the FMIP, sought to emulate business practice and to inject 'contestability' into the funding and provision of government services (Campbell 2001; Wanna and Kelly 2004). The main directions—purchaser-provider mechanisms for public services, an outcomes and outputs budgeting framework, the implementation of accrual accounting, and the augmentation of devolved purchasing authority to government agencies—were initiated by the design influences of the externally appointed National Commission of Audit, which reported on the functions and performance of the federal public sector in the government's first year (NCA 1996). There are three core components of these system changes.

First of these was a *legislative overhaul* that exchanged a financial framework dating largely from the early 1900s with a dual structure that accommodated both streamlined financial accountabilities of budget sector departments (*Financial Management and Accountability Act 1997*) and the private sector aligned standards of corporatized government entities (*Commonwealth Authorities and Companies Act 1997*). Most prominently, the former specified the individual 'entity' financial stewardship responsibilities of department heads. In conjunction with adjusted budgeting and appropriations procedures (see below), the new legislative framework accelerated the Finance Department's adoption of a 'minimalist' regulatory posture that sought to devolve to departments and agencies centralized functions like estimates preparation and appropriations controls (Blondal et al. 2008).

The second set of changes was the *outcomes and outputs budgeting framework* which from 1999 effectively replaced the PMB system (Boxall 1998; DoFA 1998; Hawke and Wanna 2010). The new system, which drew inspiration from 'contract' budget arrangements already in place in New Zealand and the Australian state of Victoria, aimed to reposition the budget process as a 'purchaser-provider' regime, prizing open public service provision to competitive pressure, and creating funding incentives for departments to operate as autonomous business entities (Robinson 2002a). The new process emphasized the outcome specification roles of ministers, who in turn took counsel from their departments on the outputs required to attain those outcomes in terms of quantity, quality, and price. The outputs subsequently 'purchased' by government were detailed in the budget documents as the planned use of appropriations. 'Business autonomy' required departments to treat budget funding for 'purchase contracts' as revenue and to compare it with the actual cost of output delivery, and in doing so replicate the 'profit-loss' measure of businesses. Crucially, one of the residual regulatory roles of the Department of Finance was to review output 'prices' to evaluate the cost basis and competitiveness of agency outputs with reference to other, usually private sector providers.

Quite sweeping changes were made to the *appropriations* process to complete the 'market-like' conditions for the new budget framework, the third reform set. First was the supplanting of traditional cash budgeting by accrual reporting and budgeting (Barton 2007). The shift to accrual budgeting—which entailed departments being funded for cash and noncash costs *incurred* in the budget period rather than simply the cash costs falling due—was the informational groundwork for more accurate costing and pricing of outputs and the valuation and management of the government's vast holdings of noncash assets and liabilities. In light of its standing in private sector accounting practice, accruals also relayed a powerful cultural signal to public servants about the mainstreaming of public sector financial management.

These changes to the accounting basis were accompanied by reorganization of the basis of appropriations (DoFD 2011; Hawke 2007). Consistent with the outcomes and outputs framework, the program structure of parliamentary votes was rendered as appropriations to high level 'outcomes', with the applicable purchased outputs enumerated in ancillary budget documents. As outcomes coincided with individual departments, in practice the new framework replaced the portfolio budgeting system. To harmonize with accruals, running and program costs were reconfigured as departmental items (discretionary operating expenses controlled by a department) and administered items (nondiscretionary expenses administered on behalf of government for program delivery).[5] This distinction reproduced the *intent* of the running cost system and framed the flexibility envisioned for transfers: departments were permitted to shift departmental appropriations across both outputs and outcomes, but administered appropriations could not be transferred across outcomes. Furthermore, because accrual appropriations now funded noncash costs—most controversially asset depreciation—departmental appropriations became *nonlapsing* to allow agencies to retain cash balances for use in future budget years.

The fundamental components of the Howard era budget reforms remained in place until quite recently, although they were amended significantly in the wake of disapproving external review, most notably the concerns of successive parliamentary inquiries about the understandability of budget information (JCPAA 2002; SSCFPA 2007; ANAO 2007) and the subsequent introduction by the first Rudd Labor Government (2007–2010) of the aptly named 'operation sunlight' reform initiative (Tanner 2008; Murray 2008). The more prominent variations—or, more accurately, reversals—included the termination of funding for non-cash expenses, the abandonment of the 'purchaser-provider' model for funding public services based on output pricing, and the reinstatement of program reporting in budget documents. The extent and longevity of these rule modifications, including any tendencies to 'revert to mean' around the general rules, can be illustrated by re-examining the impacts of the contemporary reform period through a selection of the four legacy reforms introduced earlier.

## 5.3 Legacy Reforms: Divergence and Convergence Around the General Rules

The modification of budget rules in the Australian case has, by and large, concentrated on reworking conditions within government that are said to frame flexibility. Specifically, the Howard era reforms proceeded by taking the flexibility 'gains' of earlier reform periods as settled, and, in doing so, generated unintended consequences that required the devolutionary *intent* of legacy reforms to be recovered. This points to the 'structural' and 'cultural' influences of the general budget rules; it also assists in explaining some of the consequences of the post-1999 reforms and contextualizing the variety of responses currently being implemented by the Department of Finance under the new *Public Governance, Performance and Accountability Act 2013* (CFAR 2012a, 2012b; JCPAA 2013). The four legacy reforms, and the way in which the general budget rules apply to them, are summarized in Table 5.1 below. The discussion that follows will focus on two of these reforms: program budgeting (program management and budgeting) and the running costs system.

The program management and budgeting (PMB) system was effectively the Australian version of a budget program structure tied to a performance management control system. Its key purposes were to categorize organizational expenditure as measurable objectives, including the aggregation

**Table 5.1** Types and continuity of legacy reforms: Australian budget reform 1983 to 2010

| *Reform* | *Modernized budget model (1983–1999)* | *Contemporary budget model (1999–2010)* | *Relevant general budget rules* |
|---|---|---|---|
| Program budgeting | Program management and budgeting<br>Funds appropriated to programs and accompanied by performance information<br>Basic program structure for Budget reporting | Outputs and outcomes budget framework<br>Funds appropriated to purchase outputs to achieve outcomes<br>Output performance tightly specified<br>Agencies to operate as autonomous business entities within a 'market' setting | Rule 1. Who can spend<br>Rule 3. What it can be spent on<br>Rule 5. How spending can be changed<br>Rule 6. How spending is accounted for |
| Running costs system | Aggregation of operating expenses into a single appropriation<br>Greater flexibility for program managers to reallocate inputs within programs<br>Limited carryover of unused funds and bring forward of future funds | Accrual budgeting and reporting replace cash budgeting<br>Appropriations restructured as departmental items (running costs) and administered items (program costs)<br>Appropriations for departmental items are nonlapsing | Rule 2. How much can be spent<br>Rule 4. When it must be spent<br>Rule 5. How spending can be changed |
| Portfolio budgeting | Framework for devolving budget decisions from Cabinet to Portfolio Ministers<br>Budget ceilings set for newly consolidated portfolios<br>Trade-off budget system requiring Portfolio Ministers to identify program savings to offset new spending | New legislative framework devolved financial management stewardship to department heads<br>Focus on budgeting and budget performance at the individual entity level | Rule 1. Who can spend<br>Rule 3. What it can be spent on<br>Rule 5. How spending can be changed |
| Forward estimates | Multiyear planning process to 'frame' the annual portfolio budgeting process<br>Use of rolling projections of government revenues and expenditures on a 'no policy change' basis | Medium-term expenditure framework in conjunction with new fiscal rules<br>Use of accrual reporting to manage expenses and balance sheet over a multiyear planning period | Rule 4. When it must be spent<br>Rule 5. How spending can be change<br>Rule 6. How spending is accounted for |

of detailed running cost line items, and to use program structure as the means to more closely align budget authority with managers' ability to determine how resources are deployed. Referencing our general budget rules (Table 4.1 in Chap. 4), PMB aimed to modify those rules relating to who can spend (accountability), what funds can be spent on (purpose), how spending can be changed (transfers), and how spending is accounted for (information). In turn, the outcomes and outputs framework modified this approach by appropriating to outcomes (in effect, high level objectives) and presenting government budget commitments as the planned purchase of specified outputs within a contestable setting. By virtue of its shift to accrual financial information, this system came to be known as 'accrual-based output budgeting' (Carlin and Guthrie 2001; Robinson 2002a, 2002b; Wanna and Kelly 2004).

In form then, the outcomes and outputs framework ought to have represented a prime instance of flexible budgeting: the 'funding' of outcomes, the rationalization of resource lines, and the expansion of budget decision authority for 'autonomous' entities. In not unimportant ways this was indeed the case, although these practices also contributed to its undoing, since the framework became a lightning rod for institutional conflict over appropriate levels of expenditure aggregation. For the parliament, an 'outcomes' appropriation strained the notion of a budget category to breaking point: executive government defined outcomes in such general terms as to be 'virtually meaningless' (Tanner 2008: 4), typified notoriously by the then Department of Employment and Workplace Relations outcome 'Higher pay, higher productivity'.[6] By attaching outcomes to individual budget entities, the appropriations system reinforced single entity accountability for outcomes that overlapped organizational boundaries (despite budget procedures that were intended to permit agencies to seek pooled funding for 'shared' outcomes: see MAC 2004: 76–79; CFAR 2012a: 35–37). This situation was exacerbated because the information on outputs, which was intended to provide more detail on the operational purpose of outcomes funding, was 'indicative only', and often accompanied by poor quality performance indicators that were not the product of an embedded performance management culture, as had been intended by the FMIP in the mid-to-late 1980s (ANAO 2007: 70–75).

Therefore, from a parliamentary perspective, the framework provided executive government with *too much* flexibility: 'there has actually been a regression in detail relating to programs' reported the key oversight committee, and there 'would be considerable benefit in agencies providing more disaggregated output information to support transparency and accountability for performance' (JCPAA 2002: v) (as indeed was to happen by the end of the decade). The 'flexibility' intended by outcomes appropriations was underpinned by the nonlapsing of departmental appropriations which, in principle, permitted agencies to carryover unspent cash allocations and conceivably commit those resources to activities not specifically authorized by Parliament. In general institutional terms, the framework had produced a 'control-flexibility' imbalance which was eventually met by a return to more highly prescribed purpose and informational requirements for programs, that is, tighter rules around purpose and amount.

The running costs system, which acted as a lubricant to the mechanics of PMB, was calculated to consolidate funding for administrative costs into a single appropriation and to permit departments to carry over a proportion of unused funds into later budget periods. Initially, 'running costs' were distinguished from the funding allocated for grants, subsidies or other types of services. Thereafter, under accrual-based appropriations, running and program costs were reorganized as departmental and administered expenses. Departmental expenses became nonlapsing to allow agencies to retain cash balances for application in later budget years, although administered expenses, which are limited by statutory eligibility criteria, continued to lapse at year's end. These nonlapsing provisions replaced the more limited carryover arrangements of the previous running costs system. Referring to our general budget rules, the running costs system (and its successors) was designed to modify those rules relating to how much could be spent (amount), when it must be spent (time), and how spending can be changed (transfers).

At least as it applied to a specified category of appropriations, the nonlapsing of departmental expenses sought to eliminate annuality as a constraint. Like the aggregation issues attending outcomes, the parliament was highly critical of executive government's ability under the new system to retain 'underspends' almost indefinitely, which was framed by oversight committees as a malfunctioning of both parliamentary control and finance ministry supervision (the latter for the reason that internal accounting for retained balances had been largely decentralized) (Murray 2008: 36–37). Even more pointed, however, are recent remarks by the Department of Finance that nonlapsing appropriations have *not* significantly expanded the level of agency use of carryovers for departmental appropriations (see CFAR 2012a: 46). This can in part be explained by the obstacles potentially created by the interaction between accounting and budget management rules—accounting regulations require spending amounts in future years without a matching revenue to be recognized as a 'loss', while budget management procedures require agencies to seek Department of Finance's approval to recognize the loss—but appears also to reveal an entrenched acceptance by public managers of *the felt need to manage to annual budgets.* Simply put, there remains a widespread disinclination to use carryover provisions. This has prompted a reconsideration of the status of nonlapsing provisions for annual appropriations, as well as related proposals to revert to cash appropriations, as an avenue for resolving the uncertainties and imputed disincentives associated with accounting and budget rules (CFAR 2012b: 39). As we noted regarding the behavioral impacts of resource accounting in the UK central government (see earlier discussion in Chap. 4), the annuality form of the time rule continues therefore to also cast a long shadow within the Australian case.

## Notes

1. The Department of Finance is the central finance agency that coordinates the expenditure side of the budget and manages the financial management framework of the Australian Government. During the period we survey, the department underwent several name changes to reflect enlarged functional responsibilities. We will use its basic (and current) moniker, the Department of Finance (or simply Finance).
2. Although for a more critical perspective on the coherence and intentionality of the Australian reforms see Wanna (2015).
3. The OECD (2012) and the World Bank (2013) estimate that approximately 90 per cent of high-income and middle-income countries around the world have implemented some form of MTEF.
4. The Treasury was one of the original departments of state created at the time of federation in 1901. In 1976 the Fraser Coalition Government split the department to create separate agencies for economic policy (Treasury) and budgeting and finance (Department of Finance).
5. Note that, on average, the discretionary departmental component comprised about 20 per cent of agency budgets while the nondiscretionary administered component accounted for the remaining 80 per cent. Further, three-quarters of the administered component was 'locked-in' as special appropriations, such as eligibility-based transfer payments, and excluded from the annual budget process. These special appropriations are themselves a significant form of 'inflexibility' in government budgeting.
6. Notorious because this particular outcome was the subject of a landmark legal case on the meaning of 'purpose' for Section 81 appropriations under the Australian Constitution. When in 2005 the Howard Coalition

Government launched an advertising campaign to promote its new industrial relations laws, the Australian Council of Trade Unions and the Australian Labor Party challenged the lawfulness of the campaign spending on the basis that the schedules to the Appropriation Acts had not specified it as a 'departmental item' relating to the 'outcome' appropriation. The High Court of Australia ruled that an 'outcome', irrespective of how broadly defined it was, constituted a 'purpose' and that departmental items need not be tied to that outcome (Combet v Commonwealth 2005 221 ALR 621).

## References


ANAO (Australian National Audit Office). 2007. *Application of the outcomes and outputs framework*. Audit Report No. 23 2006-07. Canberra: ANAO.

Aucoin, P. 1990. Administrative reform in public management: Paradigms, principles, paradoxes and pendulums. *Governance* 3(2): 115–137.

Barton, A. 2007. Accrual accounting and budgeting systems issues in Australian governments. *Australian Accounting Review* 17(1): 38–50.

Blondal, J.R. 2003. Budget reform in OECD member countries: Common trends. *OECD Journal on Budgeting* 2(4): 7–26.

Blondal, J.R., D. Bergvall, I. Hawkesworth, and R. Deighton-Smith. 2008. Budgeting in Australia. *OECD Journal on Budgeting* 8(2): 1–64.

Boxall, P. 1998. Outcomes and outputs: The new resource management framework. *Canberra Bulletin of Public Administration* 88: 39–43.

Campbell, C. 2001. Juggling inputs, outputs and outcomes in the search for policy competence: Recent experience in Australia. *Governance* 14(2): 253–282.

Campbell, C., and J. Halligan. 1992. *Political leadership in an age of constraint: Bureaucratic politics under Hawke and Keating*. Sydney: Allen & Unwin.

Carlin, T., and J. Guthrie. 2001. Lessons from Australian and New Zealand experiences with accrual based output budgeting systems. In *Learning from international public management reform*, vol. II, ed. L. Jones, J. Guthrie, and P. Steane, 89–100. New York: JAI Press.

CFAR (Commonwealth Financial Accountability Review). 2012a. *Is less more? Towards better Commonwealth performance*. Discussion Paper. Canberra: Department of Finance and Deregulation.

CFAR. 2012b. *Sharpening the focus: A framework for improving Commonwealth performance*. Position Paper. Canberra: Department of Finance and Deregulation.

Common, R. 1998. The new public management and policy transfer: The role of international organisations. In *Beyond the new public management: Changing ideas and practices in governance*, ed. M. Minogue, C. Polidano, and D. Hulme, 59–75. Cheltenham: Edward Elgar.

Cutt, J. 1983. The evolution of expenditure budgeting in Australia. *Public Budgeting & Finance* 3(2): 7–27.

Davis, G., and E. Craswell. 1994. The search for policy coordination: Ministerial and bureaucratic perceptions of agency amalgamations in a federal parliamentary system. *Policy Studies Journal* 22(1): 59–73.

Di Francesco, M. 1998. The measure of policy? Evaluating the evaluation strategy as an instrument for budgetary control. *Australian Journal of Public Administration* 57(1): 33–48.

DiMaggio, P.J., and W.W. Powell. 1983. The iron cage revisited: Institutional isomorphism and collective rationality in organizational fields. *American Sociological Review* 48(2): 147–160.

DoFA (Department of Finance and Administration). 1998. *Specifying outcomes and outputs: Implementing the Commonwealth's accrual-based outcomes and outputs framework*. Canberra: DoFA.

DoFD (Department of Finance and Deregulation). 2011. *The Commonwealth's appropriation framework: An introduction*. http://www.finance.gov.au/budget/budget-process/appropriation-bills.html.

Groenewegen, P. 1973. The Australian budget process. *Australian Journal of Public Administration* 32(3): 251–267.

Hawke, L. 2007. Performance budgeting in Australia. *OECD Journal on Budgeting* 7(3): 1–16.

Hawke, L., and J. Wanna. 2010. Australia after budgetary reform: A lapsed pioneer or decorative architect? In *The reality of budgetary reform in OECD nations: Trajectories and consequences*, ed. J. Wanna, L. Jensen, and J. De Vries, 65–90. Cheltenham: Edward Elgar.

Holmes, M., and D. Shand. 1995. Management reform: Some practitioner perspectives on the past ten years. *Governance* 8(5): 551–578.

JCPAA. 2013. *Advisory report on the public governance, performance and accountability bill 2013*. Report No. 438. Canberra: Parliament of Australia.

JCPAA (Joint Committee of Public Accounts and Audit). 2002. *Review of the accrual budget documentation*. Report No. 388. Canberra: Parliament of Australia.

Keating, M., and M. Holmes. 1990. Australia's budgetary and financial management reforms. *Governance* 3(2): 168–185.

Kelly, J., and J. Wanna. 2001. Are Wildavsky's guardians and spenders still relevant? New public management and the politics of government budgeting. In *Learning from international public management reform: Volume IIB*, ed. L. Jones, J. Guthrie, and P. Steane, 589–614. London: Elsevier.

MAB-MIAC (Management Advisory Board/Management Improvement Advisory Committee). 1991. *Devolution and regional offices*. Report No. 2. Canberra: AGPS.

MAB-MIAC 1993. *The Australian public service reformed: An evaluation of a decade of management reform*. Canberra: AGPS.

MAC (Management Advisory Committee). 2004. *Connecting government: Whole of government responses to Australia's priority challenges.* Canberra: MAC.

Mackay, K. 2011. The performance framework of the Australian government 1987 to 2011. *OECD Journal on Budgeting* 11(3): 75–122.

Mulgan, R. 2008. The accountability priorities of Australian parliamentarians. *Australian Journal of Public Administration* 67(4): 457–469.

Murray, A. 2008. *Review of operation sunlight: Overhauling budgetary transparency.* Canberra: Senate of the Parliament of Australia.

NCA (National Commission of Audit). 1996. *Report to the Commonwealth government.* Canberra: AGPS.

OECD. 2007. *Performance budgeting in OECD countries.* Paris: OECD.

OECD. 2012. *OECD international database of budget practices and procedures.* http://www.oecd.org/gov/budgeting.

Pollitt, C., and G. Bouckaert. 2004. *Public management reform: A comparative analysis*, 2nd ed. Oxford: Oxford University Press.

RCAGA (Royal Commission on Australian Government Administration). 1976. *Report.* Canberra: AGPS.

Robinson, M. 2002a. Financial control in Australian government budgeting. *Public Budgeting & Finance* 22(1): 80–93.

Robinson, M. 2002b. Output-purchase funding and budgeting systems in the public sector. *Public Budgeting & Finance* 22(4): 17–33.

Rothman, G., and B. Thornton. 1990. Management of budgetary expenditures: The Commonwealth running costs system. In *Budgetary management and control: The public sector in Australasia*, ed. J. Forster and J. Wanna, 92–102. Melbourne: Macmillan.

Rubin, I., and J. Kelly. 2005. Budget and accounting reforms. In *The Oxford handbook of public management*, ed. E. Ferlie, L.E. Lynn, and C. Pollitt, 563–590. Oxford: Oxford University Press.

Ruffner, M., and J. Sevilla. 2004. Public sector modernisation: Modernising accountability and control. *OECD Journal on Budgeting* 4(2): 123–141.

SCFPA (Standing Committee on Finance and Public Administration). 1990. *Not dollars alone: Review of the financial management improvement program.* Canberra: AGPS.

Schick, A. 1990. Budgeting for results: Recent developments in five industrialized countries. *Public Administration Review* 50(1): 26–34.

SSCFPA (Senate Standing Committee on Finance and Public Administration). 2007. *Transparency and accountability of Commonwealth public funding and expenditure.* Canberra: Parliament of Australia.

Tanner, L. 2008. *Operation sunlight: Enhancing budget transparency.* Canberra: Statement by the Minister for Finance and Deregulation.

Van Dooren, W., G. Bouckaert, and J. Halligan. 2015. *Performance management in the public sector*, 2nd ed. London: Routledge.

Wanna, J. 2015. Through a glass darkly: The Vicissitudes of budgetary reform in Australia. In *New accountabilities, new challenges*, ed. J. Wanna, E.A. Lindquist, and P. Marshall, 159–187. Canberra: ANU Press.

Wanna, J., and J. Kelly. 2004. Crashing through with accrual-output price budgeting in Australia. *The American Review of Public Administration* 34(1): 99–111.

Wanna, J., J. Kelly, and J. Forster. 2000. *Managing public expenditure in Australia*. Sydney: Allen & Unwin.

Weller, P., and J. Cutt. 1976. *Treasury control in Australia*. Sydney: Novak Publishing.

World Bank. 2013. *Beyond the annual budget: Global experience with medium term expenditure frameworks*. Washington, DC: World Bank.

Zifcak, S. 1994. *New managerialism: Administrative reform in Whitehall and Canberra*. Buckingham: Open University Press.

CHAPTER 6

# Calibrating Budget Flexibility and Control: A New Role for Rule Variability

**Abstract** This chapter assesses the practical opportunities that are available to reformers to better calibrate budget flexibility and control. It articulates the role of 'rule variability' as the institutionalized capacity to vary the way rules are applied within basic rule sets and explores this approach in the evolving context of the regulatory relationship between central finance agencies and spending departments. The chapter examines two conventional role types for the central finance agency ('command-and-control' and 'facilitator') and two quite radical role types ('sanctioned rule-breaking' and earned autonomy as a form of 'responsive regulation'). The chapter appraises each role type in terms of its capacity to optimize flexibility and speculates on the potential for a distinct 'rule variability' approach to budget flexibility.

Much of the foregoing discussion has traversed the budget environs in and around the center of executive government, with a focus on Westminster-style parliamentary systems. In this context, the budget and financial management system can be likened to a network of institutional roles, rule settings, and cultural dispositions, the hub of which is the central finance agency (CFA or Finance). As the 'guardian of the purse', the CFA has historically used its procedural power to exert significant influence not only in the realm of finances but also over the direction and content of public policy more generally (Wanna 2003: xxiii–xxx). As we will see, while this vector of influence has been disrupted somewhat by the effects of budget modernization (explored in the previous chapter), the power of budget



M. Di Francesco, J. Alford, *Balancing Control and Flexibility in Public Budgeting*, DOI 10.1007/978-981-10-0341-7_6

process continues to manifest itself through the one-to-many relationship between the CFA and the array of spending departments and agencies. Several different and partially contending imperatives impinge on this relationship. One of these is the public finance norm of 'budget unity': although it comprises multiple parts, government as a whole has a unified perspective on the budgeting system, as terms like 'the Budget' and 'consolidated revenue' signal (CFAR 2012a: 2). On behalf of government, the CFA and its procedural apparatus exert 'collective' financial power, aggregating tax and other revenues within its jurisdiction, and determining how and to what extent they are allocated to the various purposes instituted through departments and agencies.

In making these decisions, governments will inevitably have several and shifting concerns for the *fiscus*. One is the share of public expenditure relative to the economy as a whole. At some times, government may seek to expand public outlays to prime the economy, while at others it may strive to rein in spending to reduce a burgeoning deficit. At the same time, it may be intent on pursuing major policy initiatives in particular directions while scaling down others, for example by shifting expenditure between sectors. Moreover, as we have emphasized, having made these decisions about the size or programmatic content of its spending, government needs to ensure that they are more or less faithfully executed, thereby requiring a system of financial reporting through which departments account for the money they have been allocated.

But spending departments and agencies have differing imperatives. 'The Budget' constitutes a commitment to them that a certain level and distribution of funding is more or less guaranteed. Having received a particular allocation for defined purposes, departmental management can proceed to operate—to pay staff, buy services and disperse monies to beneficiaries—with a degree of confidence that the requisite funding is available. At the same time, however, they may find that the need for services expands or contracts unexpectedly (for example, as natural disasters hit hard or numbers of sea-borne asylum seekers dramatically expand), rendering their allocated budgets either partially redundant or woefully insufficient. In these circumstances, as we have seen, it makes sense for agencies to transfer allocations from one time period or program to another. Or, as both the asylum-seeker and natural-disaster examples also attest, several agencies may need to collaborate on a multidimensional problem, which also demands the pooling or reallocation of funds among agencies. Thus CFAs need to safeguard governments' corporate interests—such as the overall level and purposes of spending, and the public's confidence in the integrity of public finances—in a context where spending departments (and their ministers) might have good reasons, prompted by an equally valid conception of the public interest, to deviate from the intent of the whole government.

## 6.1 The Central Finance Agency: Rules and Institutional Roles

Earlier we described the way in which the various responses to nonroutine problems require some flexibility in the structures and processes of government. These responses tend to have a different logic to the standard operating procedures of government, whose 'inflexibility' is often associated with the derided concept of 'red tape' in bureaucratic organizations. While we tend to define red tape as a surfeit of pointless rules, in practice its complexion is determined more by perception, framed by the functional role and institutional location of the beholder. For example, one person's due process may be another person's vexatious constraint (Kaufman 1977).

The concept of red tape can also be used to illuminate ways in which rules assist (or hinder) 'organizational effectiveness', especially by focusing on how *rule interaction* affects the intended purpose of rules. Bozeman (2000) and Bozeman and Feeny (2011) have proposed a twofold typology of rule dysfunctionality: rules that are 'born bad' are termed 'rule-inception red tape', such as those that generate unintended consequences through faulty understanding of behavioral responses. 'Rule-evolved red tape' means rules that 'go bad' over time, such as the gradual accretion of rules that render the costs of compliance so high they result in organizational paralysis. In short, and consistent with our budget rules framework, the intent of rules and the way they interact—as well as the motives and priorities of actors who either enforce or comply with them—are all important for understanding the role of rules. In the context of public budgeting, rules are shaped by two inherent features: financial control as democratic accountability and the symbiotic relationship between CFAs and spending departments.

We have already canvassed the first of these in some detail (see Chaps. 1 and 4). We need only note here that the routines of public budgeting and financial management are located within a broader institutional framework of government accountability. In particular, the principle of annual appropriation is cemented through constitutional arrangements as not only the foundation for the accountability of executive government, but also (through 'confidence and supply') the very basis for government formation (Funnell et al. 2012).

The second defining feature in the public budget context is the way routines shape the institutional roles and responsibilities of core budget actors in executive government. CFAs and spending departments assume distinct 'rationing' and 'claiming' roles in budgeting: CFAs as 'guardians' protect the public purse, and the line department 'spenders' try to increase or protect sectoral spending (Wildavsky 1979). Budget routines reinforce these binary roles in two ways. Budgeting is a process of mutual adjustment characterized by distinct techniques of competition: guardians determine and enforce decision processes, and spenders deploy policy and operational expertise to influence the outcomes. At the same time these formal rules of budgeting are reinforced by shared cultural understandings—the closed 'budgetary village'—that allow guardians to exercise oversight through a combination of continuous assessment of spending departments' 'reputations' (Heclo and Wildavsky 1974), and 'negotiated discretion' (Thain and Wright 1995). Over time these techniques and cultural attitudes have been entrenched as budget process routines. They ultimately manage conflict by narrowing budget decisions to small changes—that is, they manifest as 'incremental budgeting'.

As noted earlier, during the 1980s and 1990s, the routines and cultures characterizing public budgeting came to be seen as a root cause of public sector growth and inefficiency. Key to the institutional response was the ability of guardians to deploy budget reform as procedural power. They used three strategies: centralizing the setting of expenditure ceilings (while excluding spenders from these processes); decentralizing responsibility for allocative decisions within the ceilings to spenders; and promoting the use of contracting and performance specification for public service delivery (this diminished spenders' capacity to argue from expertise) (Kelly and Wanna 2001: 594–604). While these changes were intended primarily to force spenders to take on 'rationing' responsibilities, they also disoriented CFAs, who were now under pressure to shift from a control-oriented 'command post' to a managerial-oriented 'strategic advisor' (Schick 2001).

The inflexibility ascribed to rules in government reflects the perspective and location of organizational actors and is framed by basic system characteristics that *embed* very strong institutional roles and *impose* accountabilities for detailed regularity. There are valid reasons for line departments to seek flexibility, but there are equally good reasons for CFAs to exercise control. For these contending priorities to be reconciled, Finance as the custodian of the financial management system must set the terms of reconciliation in the structures and rules it establishes. To a considerable degree, they can be resolved. It has long been understood by regulatory agencies, whose job is to ensure that a particular population behaves consistently with public purposes, that there is a variety of means by which an agency like Finance can bring about that behavior. Here we formulate these different approaches into four models.

## 6.2 Conventional Role Types: Command-and-Control and Facilitator

As we have seen, historically the chief model for influencing spending departments' behavior has been for Finance to act as a *command-and-control regulator*, with strictly enforced rules to limit discretion with and within spending departments (see, for example, Heclo and Wildavsky 1974; Weller and Cutt 1976). Typically carried out in a highly adversarial manner, this technique evokes the more controlling stereotypes of regulators: the use of strict rules, closely inspecting agencies' financial behaviors, detecting breaches, and applying sanctions, all reinforced by the CFA's capacity to impose obligations *before* the fact rather than in response to procedural transgressions. The preemptive method of control makes it difficult for departments to break rules even if it were inclined; the relevant transactions are controlled by Finance, with no leeway for varying them in its favor. This system inhibits flexibility in the ways we have already discussed.

One alternative to 'command-and-control' has already been widely adopted through New Public Management: *performance control.* NPM's insistence on the achievement of mandated results along with its pragmatism about how those results might be attained allows flexibility in *how* things are done (OECD 2003; Van Dooren et al. 2015: 86–116). Thus, it entails not so much greater overall flexibility as it does flexibility in respect of means rather than ends. Because outcomes are mandated, the line department has *less flexibility.* To put it another way, both command-and-control and performance control create silos, but the silos in one are different from those in the other.

But alongside these conventional models, alternative approaches are conceivable and have been emerging in practice. They are aimed at enhancing flexibility while ensuring the maintenance of the accountability and probity that have always been crucial in public budgeting processes. One of these, appearing at the opposite end of the spectrum from command-and-control regulation, is where Finance acts as an *encourager/facilitator*. The various controls exercised by the CFA are minimized, and there is greater emphasis on encouraging departments to comply voluntarily with budget rules. This has occurred mainly through the transformative role CFAs have played in leading public sector modernization. Here Finance's role is not to coerce agencies into meeting their obligations, but rather to educate, persuade, and even facilitate their compliance. In its most developed form, this entails fostering a culture in which opportunistic evasion of their obligations is widely frowned upon. As we saw earlier, between the mid-1980s and mid-2000s CFAs used budget reform to promote broader 'management improvement' efforts focused on devolving financial authority, as well as greater fiscal discipline. They integrated budgets with management, streamlined accountability arrangements, and often offered capacity-building services. This shift in budget control posture required significant *internal* cultural change in CFAs; central budget officials often struggled with the new reality that managerial leadership and advice was no substitute for the blunt authority of financial limits (Schick 2001: 9–14).

Having said this, it is also likely that such role changes have had some positive effect on the willingness and capability of spending departments to comply with the new budgeting rules. But without enforcement measures, such a model has scant chance *in itself* of ensuring that financial management within public sector organizations will operate in accordance with budget system requirements. Without some means of surveilling and enforcing departments' degree of compliance, there will always be a temptation for at least some to take advantage of the laxity of the system and divert resources from what was authorized. Equally, in the face of this behavior CFAs may lapse into the control mentality that defines their traditional place in government. Instead of seeking to encourage and assist agencies to conform to the rules, a second approach is to acknowledge that there are times when variations in the rules themselves are required to pursue the public interest. This is where Finance takes the role of negotiator.

## 6.3 Nascent Role Types: Sanctioned Rule-Breaking and Responsive Regulation

### 6.3.1 *Type 1: Sanctioned Rule-Breaking*

In earlier discussion, we saw how the conventional organizational design in the public sector—bureaucracy—sought to maximize consistency and minimize corruption, both of which were the dominant objectives of public administration for many years. In such organizations, control is usually exercised by direct oversight and strict rule application to limit discretion at lower levels of management. In this way, bureaucracies are often said to be inflexible *precisely* because in conditions of nonroutine problems managers are expected to exercise control by either applying existing rules (which may be inappropriate in the circumstances) or developing ever more detailed rules, which has long been recognized as the organizational pathology of 'trained incapacity' (for the classic account see Merton 1957; cf. Hogwood and Peters 1985: 38–55).

Of course while the public sector modernization of the 1980s and 1990s sought to remake institutions, the stark reality is that many of these organizations retain defining characteristics of large-scale bureaucracies.[1] Acknowledging this situation is actually quite critical because it suggests there are deep-seated structural and cultural aspects of bureaucratic control that are common to most—if not all—*currently conceivable* organizational forms.[2] In the search for alternate ways of balancing control and flexibility in public budgeting, it may be helpful to explore paths different to the types of restructuring that aim simply to weed out proceduralism, which (as we have already encountered in the shape of performance control) is no less a form of procedural control (Hood et al. 1999: 191–195). If, as we have suggested, flexibility may be conceived as a response capacity dependent in part on the scope of managerial discretion, another angle may be to reappraise the dual tendencies within bureaucratic structure for both inflexibility and flexibility.

One starting point is to reconsider how flexibility, at least in the terms we defined it earlier, can coincide with the very source of inflexibility in bureaucracies, formal rules. From this perspective, public servants have always been observed to display 'flexibility' whenever they exercise discretion to adjust and redefine rules or vary the way rules are interpreted and applied. This can be illustrated neatly by the apocryphal case of a police officer stopping a speeding driver and then, upon learning a pregnant passenger is in labor, actively assisting them with their passage to hospital. In this way 'rule modification'—bending or changing rules and how they are applied—can potentially be beneficial for organizational effectiveness in much the same way that most of the conventional critique of bureaucracy is cast in terms of how unthinking 'rule following' can displace or subvert substantive goals. This is an angle on bureaucratic dynamics that has a venerable scholarly history, ranging from system theory accounts of how government departments distribute control through hierarchies of 'self-correcting' organizational parts (for example, Dunsire 1978) to the grittier policy implementation tradition that focuses on 'street level bureaucrats' and the critical mediating role they play when exercising professional discretion in their treatment of clients (for instance, Lipsky 1980; also Cohen 1970).

Of most interest in this regard is the very recent exploration of the role of appropriate rule-breaking as a distinct feature of control capacity within bureaucracies, what organizational psychologists might label 'pro-social rule-breaking' (Dahling et al. 2012). From this perspective, the flexibility of an organization can be gauged by the way its structure, systems, and culture balance the tension between efficiency (the standardization benefits of general rules) and effectiveness (the customization benefits of the way specific rules are applied); in other words the extent to which an organization can:

> *tolerate* decisions by individuals to respond to a given situation in a way that is not consistent with the prescriptions of the formal policies and procedures–and in doing so, to allow for better outcomes and organizational learning without jeopardizing the integrity of the system as a whole. (Joyce et al. 2013: 3)

The degree of tolerance—used here in both the engineering sense of allowable deviation from a standard and the cultural sense of accepting difference—is the key aspect. For instance, rule-breaking can correspond with unofficial or tacit approval from rule enforcers and this can apply in different ways at different levels within an organizational hierarchy (Martin et al. 2013). As we noted in Chap. 3, case studies of collaborative working in government show time and again that this type of rule-breaking—or 'rule-bending'—is both common to and emblematic of flexible working, for example, the blind-eye that is turned at higher levels when resources are used in frontline social services for client-relevant but unsanctioned purposes. In this context, tolerance corresponds with the notion of 'workarounds': the informal, localized, and often reactive practices that, although inconsistent with rules, are nonetheless 'responsive to the underlying policy intent' (Campbell 2012: 728; cf. O'Flynn et al. 2011).

But tolerance can also work as policy through 'officially sanctioned rule-breaking'. And there is perhaps no better place to demonstrate this than the putative antithesis of public bureaucracy: a mass collaboration system. Joyce et al. (2013), for example, show how even within a purportedly 'structureless' organizational form like Wikipedia, the open-source online encyclopedia, complicated rule structures are critical to achieving shared objectives and, in particular, that these are dependent on sanctioned rule-breaking (the so-called ignore all rules policy designed to overcome procedures that are assessed as hindering either the maintenance or improvement of Wikipedia as an authoritative source of factual information). Under these arrangements, approved rule-breaking is a normalized aspect of governance, intended to act as a 'relief mechanism' when problems of both a routine and nonroutine nature emerge. Individuals are trusted to apply 'common sense and knowledge of [a] specific situation', and the policy explicitly recognizes the role of 'deliberation' in justifying the need to disregard particular rules (Joyce et al. 2013: 3-4).[3]

This approach compares favorably with organizational designs that seek to expand managerial discretion. It also has important implications for the way that sanctioned rule-breaking—or at least greater propensity for its tolerance—can be built into public organizational design to promote flexibility. This can operate, for example, as latitude, meaning rule systems incorporate leeway that supports rule-breaking (or rule-bending), accompanied by clearly defined decision rights in this respect. Alternatively, and perhaps more realistically, the sanctioned rule-breaking approach can work in diagnostic terms, so that when authorized as a core value of an organization rule-breaking acts as an indicator of the suitability of rule sets: the more that managers turn to 'workarounds', the less aligned specific rule sets may be with the organization's goals (Joyce et al. 2013: 9; cf. 'green tape' approaches canvassed briefly in Chap. 4).

Of course, in both cases, one of the obvious weaknesses with this method is how, precisely, to delineate and account for constructive rule-bending as opposed to merely capricious decision-making, a problem whose contours will in part be traced by the character of an organization's culture and the way it promotes trust to minimize internal and external relationship costs (Alford and O'Flynn 2012: 124–132). A public budgeting equivalent of the Wikipedia 'ignore all rules' policy is extremely unlikely, particularly in terms of the heightened political and managerial risks to which actors at various levels of government organizations would be exposed. The key suggestion here is more subtle: that rule-breaking could be repositioned within formal organizational structure, so that pro-social behavior that is currently both localized and unsanctioned is capable of being scaled up as a set of tolerance limits within organizational policy. At the very least, what is proposed is that rule-breaking in its various forms is an inherent feature of bureaucratic structure and behavior, one that perhaps should not be managed solely through opposing it. Rather, better acknowledging its place within organizational design, particularly in the way it can harness the productive capacity of discretion, may be one way—albeit quite radical—of strengthening flexibility as a control capacity. Strategies that align sanctions (or rewards) with the self-selected compliance behavior of regulatees could be a starting point for this design task.

### *6.3.2 Type 2: Responsive Regulation*

Our final alternative is *responsive regulation*. One of the most widely researched and adopted frameworks in the broader field of regulation (Ayres and Braithwaite 1992), it has received little attention in the design of regulation *within* government. Responsive regulation starts from a recognition that people comply with their regulatory obligations for a number of reasons, only one of which is the fear of punishment (others include intrinsic motivations, material incentives, social obligation, and moral values) (Alford and O'Flynn 2012: 56–82). These factors affect regulatees' *willingness* to comply. Further, people are more likely to obey rules if they feel *able* to do so, which is a function of either the simplicity of the compliance task or the capability of the regulatee. People are complex bundles of motivations and capacities, which can be grouped into a series of 'compliance postures' (Braithwaite 1995). For example, some people may adopt a posture of trying to evade their obligations whenever it is both profitable and possible, while others may be disposed to obey rules in all circumstances because they attach moral weight to lawfulness.[4] In between are varying compliance postures. For instance, what we might call 'incompetent noncompliers' who wish to comply but find it technically difficult to do so (hopefully not a problem in CFAs!), and 'contingent compliers' who will comply to the extent they see the regulator dealing with the opportunistic noncompliers and therefore do not feel like 'suckers' for having complied themselves (Alford and Speed 2006).

The point about these varying postures is that it does not make sense to apply a uniform regulatory approach across all of them. If the regulator applies only 'soft' methods such as education and persuasion, they will be insufficiently robust to influence opportunistic evaders, who will take advantage of the lax regime. But if 'hard' enforcement and compulsion is applied to all regulatees, this will alienate those with a law-abiding posture, while having minimal effect on incompetent noncompliers (who are willing to comply but find it difficult). Responsive regulation is thus a way of mixing 'punishment and persuasion' in an optimal fashion (Braithwaite 1985). Regulators need to apply different instruments to differing postures among regulatees, but this in itself presents a problem: how to decide which clients to target with which interventions?

The regulatory pyramid (see Fig. 6.1) provides an answer to this problem. It constitutes a hierarchy of regulatory instruments using 'Tit-for-Tat' strategies and is underpinned by the background possibility of heavy sanctions. The regulator begins by being 'nice' to regulatees, providing help, information, persuasion, and fair treatment. If they comply, this 'soft' approach continues, but if they take advantage of the situation by failing to comply, the regulator becomes stricter, for instance giving warnings. Again,

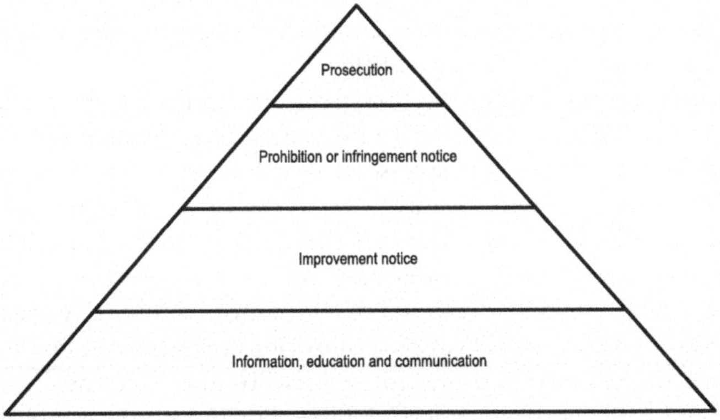


**Fig. 6.1** The responsive regulation pyramid: Hierarchy of regulatory enforcement options. *Source*: Adapted from Ayres and Braithwaite (1992): 35

if the regulatee complies, the regulator reverts to a helpful approach. But if the regulatee continually fails to comply, the regulator adopts an event stricter stance, for instance by levying a fine. These mutual responses escalate up to higher levels of the pyramid for recalcitrants, or remain lower down for those who are compliant. In consequence, over a period of time, responsive regulation 'varies' interventions in two ways. First, the regulatees effectively *select themselves* for stricter or more lenient treatment, by the way they behaved in the previous encounter; second, regulators can assess the likelihood and consequences of noncompliance based on this information and *target interventions* to those with higher risk compliance postures.

The regulatory pyramid has been applied across very different systems of government and now underpins a range of *external* regulatory functions, including corporations law, occupational health and safety, food and consumer product safety, and child protection (see Wood et al. 2010; Ivec et al. 2015). Revenue administration is one area in which emulation of the framework has been highest. Traditionally, regulation in this area is both highly routinized and heavily sanctions-based. The Australian Taxation Office (ATO) pioneered the 'cooperative compliance model' in the 1990s as a basis for interacting with individual and corporate taxpayers (Murphy 2004). It operationalizes the regulatory pyramid as a set of protocols for evaluating clients' motivations for noncompliance and applying a set of proportionate compliance strategies. The ATO subsequently used compliance data to build profiles of compliance risk and developed a range of targeted interventions. For example, its 'key client managers scheme' locates auditors within the corporate headquarters of large companies assessed as being of higher risk (Braithwaite 2005).

We believe public budgetary processes are similar to these regulatory arenas because CFAs aim to encourage spending departments' compliance with budget rules. We have seen that 'one-size-fits-all' approach is not effective for budgeting, as in other types of regulation. Neither the 'command-and-control' nor the 'encourager/facilitator' models of the CFA role are—individually—adequate to the task. But as it combines key aspects of these two, 'responsive regulation' presents greater scope for flexibility without significantly compromising government's need to account for the effectiveness and integrity of budget systems.

How could this work in practice? First, Finance could establish a core set of modified budget rules. These could further relax some of the existing controls over allocation of funds between programs, and be underpinned by the type of training and cultural change discussed above. The new rules would be complemented by Finance monitoring for a certain time period, which would involve looking at *how* line departments behave under the freer regime and *why* they do so. For instance, assessing whether departments reallocate funds between programs in a manner consistent with governmental objectives for both the relevant area and the budget overall would inform Finance's application of 'rule variability', such as continuing budget flexibility for agencies that comply with government objectives encapsulated in the rules or, for those who have not complied, selective reimposition of control by Finance proportionate to the noncompliance. All of this would constitute the basis of a systematic cycle of monitoring and negotiation overseen by Finance.[5]

## 6.4 Earned Autonomy: The Central Finance Agency as a 'Responsive Regulator'

Some CFAs in Australia and the UK have implemented, or are exploring, a variant of responsive regulation of funding systems known as *earned autonomy*, which uses tiered incentives to rate, compare, and reward or sanction regulated organizations based on assessed performance. In the UK, earned autonomy was an organizing concept underpinning the Blair Labour Government's targets-based approach to public service improvement (HM Treasury and Cabinet Office 2004). In practice, however, it was mainly applied to funding models for local government authorities and National Health Service trusts (Mannion et al. 2007). In these types of 'funder-provider' contexts, earned autonomy involved rewards for high performing organizations and interventions for low performing organizations. Performance was assessed by global ratings systems, and incentives were 'triggered' by predefined thresholds. Both of these were publicly reported. Incentives ranged from lighter touch monitoring (e.g. less frequent reporting) to increased autonomy (e.g. the removal of cost limits) and budgetary rewards (e.g. retention of proceeds from asset sales) (Mannion et al. 2007: 404). On the other hand, sanctions might include a tighter monitoring role for the funder, the installation of greater contestability or, in the worst case scenario, management removal.

In Australia, the Department of Finance's recent review of the existing sector-wide financial accountability framework has identified earned autonomy as a 'more nuanced and proportionate' alternative to the 'one-size-fits-all' approach (CFAR 2012b: 23; JCPAA 2013: 32). The Department's motivation is to construct a *financial regulatory framework* with a whole of government application. The main idea is to target compliance more carefully: a set of ***minimum*** financial management requirements would initially apply across all government departments, but this would over time lead to varying levels of oversight and intervention calibrated by Finance's assessment of each department's financial and nonfinancial risk profile and performance. One concrete way that has been flagged for applying this approach is through tiered and/or differential financial and performance reporting that is calibrated to the budget materiality, functions, and risks of reporting entities (CFAR 2012b: 35–37). Like the British model, the proposed Australian system is based on a clear link between performance and autonomy. It anticipates the need to intervene in the case of poor performance, but as its theoretical basis lies in responsive regulation, its premise is that departments 'set out to achieve results within the law and in accordance with government's policy priorities, including budgetary settings' (CFAR 2012b: 23).

In both varieties of earned autonomy, the rationale is to tie the awarding of greater budgetary freedom to prior demonstrations of trustworthiness, at least as measured by predefined performance and risk data. In this way, the spending department can demonstrate its trustworthiness and earn the right to no longer be subject to ongoing suspicion. Both contrast strongly with the command-and-control model, in which agencies are constantly subject to control founded in suspicion.

This approach can, however, be taken further. As a variation on responsive regulation, earned autonomy might also provide a template for the operational definition of 'sanctioned rule-breaking'. As we noted earlier, tacitly approved rule-breaking is often associated with flexible working, such as when staff redeploy program resources for client-responsive but unsanctioned purposes; and this, in turn, is often a function of the *level of trust* that exists between supervisors and staff within and between organizations. One measure of trust is the extent to which an organization can 'tolerate' staff decisions that depart from formal rules but can be accounted for in delivering measurably better organizational outcomes. This notion of tolerance is key. As we have seen, an earned autonomy model seeks to align regulatory requirements—for instance, delegated decision authority, central rule application, and the detail and frequency of reporting—to the risk compliance profile of an organization. Based on predefined risk and performance criteria, organizations are categorized by which rules apply to them and how; for some agencies quite basic rules prohibiting program transfers and carryovers would be applied and enforced rigorously, and for others these types of activities will be quite routine because of the operative level of trust. In this way, an earned autonomy model is *one method for laying out the 'tolerance limits' for scaled-up rule-breaking*, defined initially as sanctioned departures from minimum rule sets and ultimately assessed in the context of both financial regularity and outcomes performance. The main problems with this approach are that first, it is heavily dependent on unambiguous definitions of the notion of 'risk' in the public sector; and second, it could easily lead to unsustainable levels of differential rule application—something the Australian Parliament noted in its review of Finance's proposed earned autonomy model (see JCPAA 2013: 33–34; cf. Newberry 2013: 11)—and well beyond the monitoring capabilities of even the best resourced CFA.

We note that the application of responsive regulation *within* government has not gone completely unnoticed by scholars. It also has its critics. Some doubt that the public sector possesses the necessary cultural conditions for 'enforced self-regulation' (Hood 2004: 16–17; Hood et al. 1999: 65–67, 191–195). For example, are 'hard' sanctions credible when both regulators and regulatees can petition political superiors to stop the escalation process? More broadly, is the 'relational distance' between regulator and regulatee an insurmountable problem for responsive regulation, such that the more distant the relationship (i.e., the fewer the encounters) the less effective escalation of sanctions is likely to be? We acknowledge these concerns, but argue that responsive regulation is well equipped to deal with these kinds of problems *because* it has recourse to relational responses to areas of high risk—as discussed earlier in the case of the ATO—through the deployment of regulatory 'intermediaries' and the demonstration effect of enforcement 'surges' in high risk organizations (Braithwaite and Hong 2015).

Finally, there is a danger that the earned autonomy approach may also undermine one of the key mechanisms that animates responsive regulation: namely, that Finance's reposing of trust in the regulated department *from the outset* generates greater trust by the spending department in return. Not only is it vital that Finance be able to trust the spending department, but it is also important that the spending department can trust Finance, primarily because it is consequently more likely to divulge information to the CFA, in a virtuous circle of reciprocity (Gouldner 1960). This certainly has its equivalence in the traditional 'village culture' of central government, and the way central agencies tended to exercise oversight through 'continuous mutual assessment of ability and trustworthiness' (Hood et al. 1999: 71–73; see also Heclo and Wildavsky 1974; Thain and Wright 1995). But as an even larger literature on trust-building shows, such reciprocity is more powerfully engendered if the stance taken by each party is manifestly based less on calculation and more on 'gifts' in the true sense, that they are given without visible expectation of a quid pro quo. These gifts can be tangible or intangible, economic or noneconomic—for example, providing information, assistance in gaining access to decision-makers, cutting a service-provider some slack for being slightly behind schedule on a delivery, signaling respect, and so on. The point is that a less calculative reciprocity usually generates a more thorough form of trust, founded not so much in the cognitive recognition that the other party has no choice but to stick to 'the deal', but more in the affective feeling that the other will 'do the right thing'.

The introduction of earned autonomy as a variant of responsive regulation therefore entails a trade-off between the need to build trust between the CFA and spending departments, and the need to avoid large-scale exploitation of a freer framework, at least in the short term. In short, it calls for a more nuanced appreciation of the relative risks involved and indeed of those inherent in the other options (Barrett 2014). It also requires CFAs to consider broader, almost existential, questions about the selection, appropriateness, and mix of the 'instruments' they use for governing the budget system (Eliades et al. 2005). By way of summation, Table 6.1 below sets out a comparison of all four approaches in the terms discussed here.

**Table 6.1** Alternative approaches to the central finance agency regulatory role

| *Model* | *Impact on flexibility/ control* | *Impact on trust building* | *Risk of opportunism by line agency* |
|---|---|---|---|
| Command-and-control | Inflexible | Adverse | Low |
| Encourager/facilitator | Very flexible, but inadequate control | Positive | High |
| Responsive regulation | High levels of flexibility and control as appropriate to each line | Highly positive | Low to moderate |
| Earned autonomy | Similar to responsive regulation, but with more emphasis on control | Positive | Low |

## Notes

1. That is, formalization (the reliance on rules and procedures), specialization (the delineation of functions that require expertise), standardization (the completion of work activities in a consistent manner) and hierarchy (the vertical differentiation of decision-making authority). A similar observation could be made of large private sector organizations, regardless of their for-profit or not-for-profit status.
2. This is salient in two respects. First, arguably this observation was the key revelation residing in Max Weber's premonition of the 'rationalization' or 'iron cage' of social life (Weber 1946). Second, were bureaucracy to be likened to a type of 'genetic coding' that resides in large-scale organizational behavior, it should not escape our attention that even within respected contingency-based approaches to organizational design, 'bureaucracy' serves as the instructional basis for the range of organizational types (see, by way of example, Mintzberg 1998).
3. Tempered, of course, by the role of reputational risk for Wikipedia contributors, that is, that the need for rule-breaking must be proposed and justified in ways that are acceptable to other contributors within the Wikipedia community. This too has its equivalence in traditional public bureaucratic structures, especially the way public service 'professionalism' socializes officials and creates expectations about how they are to behave in their roles.
4. In practice, of course, many regulatees are not individuals but rather organizations, especially corporations. As a result, and while acknowledging that individual motivations are mediated by more complex factors such as structure, culture, and prior socialization processes, responsive regulation is commonly applied to organizations as well as individuals.
5. As noted earlier, this has parallels with the notion of 'negotiated discretion' in which the CFA's relationship with spending departments is contingent on a range of relational characteristics (reputation and competency) and issue salience (nature and priority of policy and financial matters) (Thain and Wright 1995: Chap. 10).

## References

Alford, J., and J. O'Flynn. 2012. *Rethinking public service delivery: Managing with external providers.* Basingstoke: Palgrave Macmillan.

Alford, J., and R. Speed. 2006. Client focus in regulatory agencies: Oxymoron or opportunity. *Public Management Review* 8(2): 313–331.

Ayres, I., and J. Braithwaite. 1992. *Responsive regulation: Transcending the deregulation debate.* New York: Oxford University Press.

Barrett, P. 2014. New development: Financial reform and good governance. *Public Money & Management* 34(1): 59–66.

Bozeman, B. 2000. *Bureaucracy and red tape*. Upper Saddle River, NJ: Prentice Hall.

Bozeman, B., and M. Feeny. 2011. *Rules and red tape: A prism for public administration research and theory*. New York: M E Sharpe.

Braithwaite, J. 1985. *To punish or persuade: Enforcement of coal mine safety*. Albany, NY: State University of New York Press.

Braithwaite, V. 1995. Games of engagement: Postures within the regulatory community. *Law and Policy* 17(3): 225–255.

Braithwaite, J. 2005. *Markets in vice, markets in virtue*. Sydney: The Federation Press.

Braithwaite, J., and S.H. Hong. 2015. The iteration deficit in responsive regulation: Are regulatory ambassadors an answer? *Regulation and Governance* 9(1): 16–29.

Campbell, D. 2012. Public managers in integrated services collaboratives: What works is workarounds. *Public Administration Review* 72(5): 721–730.

CFAR (Commonwealth Financial Accountability Review). 2012a. *Is less more? Towards better Commonwealth performance*. Discussion Paper. Canberra: Department of Finance and Deregulation.

CFAR. 2012b. *Sharpening the focus: A framework for improving Commonwealth performance*. Position Paper. Canberra: Department of Finance and Deregulation.

Cohen, H. 1970. Bureaucratic flexibility: Some comments on Robert Merton's 'Bureaucratic structure and personality'. *The British Journal of Sociology* 21(4): 390–399.

Dahling, J., S. Chau, D. Mayer, and J. Gregory. 2012a. Breaking rules for the right reasons? An investigation of pro-social rule breaking. *Journal of Organizational Behaviour* 33(1): 21–42.

Dunsire, A. 1978. *Control in a bureaucracy*. Oxford: Martin Robinson.

Eliades, P., M. Hill, and M. Howlett (eds.). 2005. *Designing government: From instruments to governance*. Montreal & Kingston: McGill-Queen's University Press.

Funnell, W., K. Cooper, and J. Lee. 2012. *Public sector accounting and accountability in Australia*, 2nd ed. Sydney: UNSW Press.

Gouldner, A. 1960. The norm of reciprocity: A preliminary statement. *American Sociological Review* 25(2): 161–178.

Heclo, H., and A. Wildavsky. 1974. *The private government of public money: Community and policy inside British politics*. London: Macmillan.

HM Treasury and Cabinet Office. 2004. *Devolving decision making. Volume 1—Delivering better public services: Refining targets and performance management*. London: HMSO.

Hogwood, B.W., and B. Guy Peters. 1985. *The pathology of public policy*. Oxford: Clarendon Press.

Hood, C. 2004. Controlling public services and government: Towards a cross-national perspective. In *Controlling modern government: Variety, commonality and change*, ed. C. Hood, O. James, B. Guy Peters, and C. Scott, 3–21. Cheltenham: Edward Elgar.

Hood, C., O. James, G. Jones, C. Scott, and T. Travers. 1999. *Regulation inside government: Waste-watchers, quality police and sleazebusters.* Oxford: Oxford University Press.

Ivec, M., V. Braithwaite, C. Wood, and J. Job. 2015. *Applications of responsive regulatory theory in Australia and overseas: Update.* Regulatory Institutions Network Occasional Paper 23. Canberra: Australian National University.

JCPAA. 2013. *Advisory report on the public governance, performance and accountability bill 2013.* Report No. 438. Canberra: Parliament of Australia.

Joyce, E., J. Pike, and B. Butler. 2013. Keeping eyes on the prize: Officially sanctioned rule breaking in mass collaboration systems. *Proceedings of the ACM conference on computer supported cooperative work and social computing (CSCW)*, San Antonio, TX, USA, 23-27 February 2013.

Kaufman, H. 1977. *Red tape: Its origins, uses and abuses.* Washington, DC: The Brookings Institution.

Kelly, J., and J. Wanna. 2001. Are Wildavsky's guardians and spenders still relevant? New public management and the politics of government budgeting. In *Learning from international public management reform: Volume IIB*, ed. L. Jones, J. Guthrie, and P. Steane, 589–614. London: Elsevier.

Lipsky, M. 1980. *Street-level bureaucracy: Dilemmas of the individual in public services.* New York: Russell Sage.

Mannion, R., M. Goddard, and A. Bate. 2007. Aligning incentives and motivations in health care: The case of earned autonomy. *Financial Accountability & Management* 23(4): 401–420.

Martin, A., S. Lopez, V. Roscignoand, and R. Hodson. 2013. Against the rules: Synthesising types and processes of bureaucratic rulebreaking. *Academy of Management Review* 38(4): 550–574.

Merton, R.K. 1957. *Social theory and social structure.* Glencoe: The Free Press.

Mintzberg, H. 1998. The structuring of organizations. In *The strategy process*, ed. H. Mintzberg, J.B. Quinn, and S. Ghoshal. New York: Prentice Hall.

Murphy, K. 2004. Moving towards a more effective model of regulatory enforcement in the Australian taxation office. *British Tax Review* 6: 603–619.

Newberry, S. 2013. *Public sector accounting and earned autonomy: Accountability lost?* Allan Barton Memorial Lecture, 2013 CPA Congress, Canberra, 16 October 2013.

O'Flynn, J., F. Buick, D. Blackman, and J. Halligan. 2011. You win some, you lose some: Experiments with joined-up government. *International Journal of Public Administration* 34(4): 244–254.

OECD (Organization for Economic Cooperation and Development). 2003. *Public sector modernization: Governing for performance.* GOV/PUMA 2003(20). Paris: OECD.

Schick, A. 2001. The changing role of the central budget office. *OECD Journal on Budgeting* 1(1): 9–26.

Thain, C., and M. Wright. 1995. *The treasury and Whitehall: The planning and control of public expenditure, 1976–1983.* Oxford: Oxford University Press.

Van Dooren, W., G. Bouckaert, and J. Halligan. 2015. *Performance management in the public sector*, 2nd ed. London: Routledge.

Wanna, J. 2003. Introduction: The changing role of central budget agencies. In *The reality of budgetary reform in OECD nations: Trajectories and consequences*, ed. J. Wanna, L. Jensen, and J. De Vries, xxiii–xxxviii. Cheltenham: Edward Elgar.

Weber, M. 1946. *From Max Weber: Essays in sociology.* Trans. and ed. H.H. Gerth and C. Wright Mills. New York: Oxford University Press.

Weller, P., and J. Cutt. 1976. *Treasury control in Australia.* Sydney: Novak Publishing.

Wildavsky, A. 1979. *The politics of the budgetary process*, 3rd ed. Boston, MA: Little Brown.

Wood, C., M. Ivec, J. Robb, and V. Braithwaite. 2010. *Applications of responsive regulatory theory in Australia and overseas.* Regulatory Institutions Network Occasional Paper 15. Canberra: Australian National University.

CHAPTER 7

# Conclusion

*We thought we were empowering people who manage things, but ended up empowering those who count things (Hood et al. 1999: 195).*

**Abstract** This chapter summarizes the potential for 'rule variability' in operationalizing the balance between central oversight for consistency and the situational need for flexibility. The incidence of nonroutine problems requires government to develop greater capacity for collaboration, which is dependent on the exercise of flexibility. By reconceptualizing budget control as a set of general rules, the scope of rule variability as a source of budget flexibility is explored in the context of the 'regulatory' relationship between central finance agencies and spending departments. The chapter emphasizes the leadership role of central finance agencies in facilitating voluntary rule compliance and the potential for new 'earned autonomy' approaches that replicate responsive regulation strategies within government.

The starting point for this book is a contention, over time emerging from those who fund as much as those who are funded, that budgeting and financial management practices within the public sector are a brake on flexibility and the type of behaviors required to manage nonroutine problems. It is, we believe, a contention that is often asserted and seldom



M. Di Francesco, J. Alford, *Balancing Control and Flexibility in Public Budgeting*, DOI 10.1007/978-981-10-0341-7_7

examined. For a start it tends to disregard a historically significant period of public sector budget modernization largely prosecuted in the name of 'devolution' and, in more recent times, facilitated through the data collection and monitoring technologies enabled by information management systems. At the very least it pays insufficient attention to how this type of rule relaxation may have inadvertently reconfigured how central control is exercised (as the epigraph above suggests). In any case, it is perhaps too simplistic a claim to make: against a backdrop of increasing policy complexity and turbulence, budget processes in government are inevitably caught between contending institutional—and community—imperatives for responsiveness and consistency. In other words, more flexibility is not necessarily an unalloyed good.

In this book, therefore, we asked the question: how can public budgeting be made more flexible without diminishing government's capacity to ensure public money is used for the purposes it has mandated? To prefigure a way forward, we proposed that the notion of 'rule variability' has significant potential in operationalizing the delicate balance between central oversight for consistency and the situational need for flexibility. The argument proceeded in four steps.

First, the incidence of 'nonroutine' problems requires government to develop greater capacity for collaboration and agility, both of which are dependent on the ability of individuals and organizations to exercise 'flexibility', especially in the way resources are allocated and accounted for. Here, flexibility can be defined as operating along two dimensions: how far down an organizational hierarchy decision-making authority is extended (devolution) and the latitude within the rules that decision-makers at different levels have to vary decisions (discretion). The further down authority is extended, and the more latitude for decision-makers to vary their responses, the more flexible a budget system can be said to be.

Second, the traditional approach to budgeting in the public sector, which equates to control of, and accountability for, financial inputs, operates through a small number of 'general rules' of budget control designed to limit discretion. Using two of the most prominent rules—when funds must be spent (annuality) and what those funds must be spent on (purpose)—we demonstrated how these rules have been internalized by relevant institutional actors and how, in the face of sustained efforts since the early-to-mid 1980s to modernize budget processes, the rules continue to exert strong influence on budgetary behavior. This was illustrated through an extended case study of the development and impact of performance-based budget reforms in the Australian federal government, as well as reportage of reform-specific experience in other jurisdictions.

Third, applying our two-dimensional definition of flexibility, we explored the scope for rule variability as a source of budget flexibility, and illustrated what 'high flexibility' for each rule might conceivably look like. High flexibility was characterized by budget authority:

- attached to a broadly defined purpose rather than simply an organizational authorization;
- delegated according to the principle of subsidiarity;
- oriented toward a process of continuous budget adjustment across multiyear periods;
- able to be defined across a range of organizational and programmatic budget categories as appropriate to different types of services and delivery modes; and
- accompanied by contingency-based information requirements where the frequency and content of reporting can be customized to organizational and programmatic circumstances.

While this characterization seemed to point to fewer rules—a relatively orthodox decentralization response—we suggested that the balance between control and flexibility may lie more in the type of rules and the ways they are applied.

Fourth, we surveyed the notion of rule variability in the context of the longstanding 'regulatory' relationship between CFAs and spending departments. In pursuing distinct institutional roles, each has valid—although contending—reasons to pursue either enhanced control or expanded flexibility. Against this background, the fundamental issue is whether CFAs have available to them the means to reconcile these legitimate expectations other than conventional 'command-and-control' and 'performance control' regulatory postures.

There are, we think, a range of regulatory options that are deserving of consideration, including the leadership role of CFAs in 'facilitating' voluntary rule compliance, as well as more speculative intervention in the way that 'sanctioned rule-breaking' could be encouraged in negotiation with trusted organizations. Potentially, both options are covered by a unifying approach that replicates 'responsive regulation' strategies within government. In this orientation, which already has its adherents in the emerging form of earned autonomy, CFAs use a graduated set of sanctions and rewards that allow regulatees to self-select their regulatory treatment. While it depends crucially on trust building, and must also be mindful that differential rule application may inevitably be subject to 'overstretch', if pursued in concert with other key monitory institutions (such as legislatures and satellite watchdog bodies), responsive regulation represents a step change in 'framing' budget and financial management within government. In this way, rule variability may be one way of configuring the budget flexibility needed to manage problems of both a routine and nonroutine nature.

## Reference

Hood, C., O. James, G. Jones, C. Scott, and T. Travers. 1999. *Regulation inside government: Waste-watchers, quality police and sleazebusters.* Oxford: Oxford University Press.

# Index



Note: Page number followed by 'n' refers to endnotes.


M. Di Francesco, J. Alford, *Balancing Control and Flexibility in Public Budgeting*, DOI 10.1007/978-981-10-0341-7

The manufacturer's authorised representative in the EU is Springer Nature Customer Service Centre GmbH, Europaplatz 3, 69115 Heidelberg, Germany. If you have any concerns regarding our products, please contact ProductSafety@springernature.com

Printed and bound by CPI Group (UK) Ltd, Croydon, CR0 4YY
22/09/2026
02221054-0016